Praise for
FREEDOM

How Teens Can Use Mindful Compassion to Thrive in a Chaotic World and Grow a Purpose-driven Life

"In *Freedom*, the authors have created a tremendous resource for adolescents who struggle with difficult emotions, shame, and insecurity. The wisdom of self-compassion is on full display here, in an easy-to-read book that is chock full of engaging personal stories, accessible information, and useful practices. Highly recommended!"

Russell Kolts, PhD

Director, Inland Northwest Compassionate Mind Center

Author of *CFT Made Simple* and *Experiencing Compassion-Focused Therapy from the Inside Out*

"I think this book has accomplished a very difficult task. The authors have managed to condense solid scientific principles into language that is accessible, interesting, and salient to adolescents. *Freedom* is absolutely jam-packed full of memorable examples and practices that teens can actually use to help them to sift through the chaos and stress of modern life and walk towards being the kind of person THEY want to be in the world, not because their parents think it's a worthwhile endeavor, but because THEY can see that this stuff really matters. Having tried out some of these practices on my own kids, I can't wait to start recommending this excellent book to all the young people who attend my clinic."

Sarah Cassidy, PhD

Senior Educational, Child, and Adolescent Psychologist at The Smithsfield Clinic, A Centre for Learning and Behaviour
Adjunct Professor of Child Counselling and Educational Psychology at Maynooth University, Ireland

Founder and Chief Education Officer at RaiseYourIQ

"*Freedom* is a fabulous book full of wisdom and warmth. I highly recommend it to anyone, young or old. We can all benefit from the skillful way in which Chris and Heather teach and demonstrate mindful compassion in this accessible and highly useful book. If you are an adolescent or know and love an adolescent, this book is for you!"

Laura Silberstein-Tirch, Psy.D.

Clinical Psychologist & Director of The Center for Compassion Focused Therapy

Adjunct Assistant Professor, at Albert Einstein School of Medicine, Yeshiva University and Author of *How to Be Nice to Yourself: The Everyday Guide to Self-Compassion: Effective Strategies to Increase Self-Love and Acceptance*

"In this excellent book, Heather and Chris take us on a warm, personal, and detailed tour of how we can transform our lives with compassion and mindfulness. Highly recommended!"

Dennis Doshin Tirch, PhD

Founding Director, The Center for Compassion Focused Therapy, New York City

Author of *The Compassionate Mind Guide to Overcoming Anxiety*

Calliope House Press — Dublin, Ohio

Printed in the United States of America.

Copyeditor: Bridie O'Shaughnessy
Cover Design: Diane Lorenzo
Front Cover Art: Heather Preston
Back Cover Art: Heather Doyle Fraser
Interior Design and Layout: Diane Six
Interior Art, Nature Series: Heather Preston
Interior Art, Hand Illustration Series: Stephen Swartz
Photo Credit (author photo): Catherine Murray

ISBN: 978-0-578-52695-9

Important Note: *This publication is designed to provide accurate, complete, and authoritative information in regard to the subject matter covered in accordance with the standards of practice that are accepted at the time of publication. However, in view of the possibility of human error or changes in behavioral, mental health, or medical sciences, neither the authors nor any other party who has been involved in the preparation or publication of this work is responsible for any errors or omissions or the results obtained from the use of such information. If expert assistance or counseling is needed, the services of a competent professional should be sought immediately.*

Calliope House Press — Dublin, Ohio

Printed in the United States of America.

Copyeditor: Bridie O'Shaughnessy
Cover Design: Diane Lorenzo
Front Cover Art: Heather Preston
Back Cover Art: Heather Doyle Fraser
Interior Design and Layout: Diane Six
Interior Art, Nature Series: Heather Preston
Interior Art, Hand Illustration Series: Stephen Swartz
Photo Credit (author photo): Catherine Murray

ISBN: 978-0-578-52695-9

Important Note: *This publication is designed to provide accurate, complete, and authoritative information in regard to the subject matter covered in accordance with the standards of practice that are accepted at the time of publication. However, in view of the possibility of human error or changes in behavioral, mental health, or medical sciences, neither the authors nor any other party who has been involved in the preparation or publication of this work is responsible for any errors or omissions or the results obtained from the use of such information. If expert assistance or counseling is needed, the services of a competent professional should be sought immediately.*

Also by
Heather Doyle Fraser

40 Weeks: A Daily Journey of
Inspiration and Abundance

40 Weeks: A Weekly Companion
Journal and Reflection Guide

Daily Gratitude and Intention Journal

FREEDOM

Chris Fraser, MSW • Heather Doyle Fraser

How Teens Can Use
Mindful Compassion
to Thrive in a Chaotic
World and Grow a
Purpose-driven Life

Table of Contents

Introduction xii

Dedication xix

Part One: The Untold Story

CH 1 - We Are All Connected 3

CH 2 - It's Not Our Fault 17

CH 3 - You Are Not Alone 39

Table of Contents

Part Two: The Practices

CH 4 - Discovering What Is Important to Me.. 59

CH 5 - Going for It!.. 75

CH 6 - Help Is on the Way 97

CH 7 - Motivating with Kindness. 123

CH 8 - What Else Can I Do? 153

CH 9 - Following the Spark 175

References & Resources 204

Acknowledgements 206

About the Authors 208

About the Artists 210

Introduction

We are so glad you have found your way to *Freedom: How Teens Can Use Mindful Compassion to Thrive in a Chaotic World and Grow a Purpose-driven Life*. Our hope is that this book becomes a haven—a safe place—for you. A place where you can be free—a place where you can be yourself and share your thoughts and feelings without judgment.

Everything about this book is set up to help you create more psychological freedom and flexibility in your life, even the cover. You will notice that the cover only has the main title on it—*FREEDOM*—and does not have our subtitle: *How Teens Can Use Mindful Compassion to Thrive in a Chaotic World and Grow a Purpose-driven Life*. This is on purpose.

Why did we not include the subtitle on the cover? This may seem to be a bit strange and also to go against every book publishing and marketing rule in existence. If you are thinking this, you are not alone! But, we know that you most likely didn't find this book on your own. An adult probably gave it to you or suggested that you read it. That in itself is probably a barrier to you reading it. But if the book also had a title and a subtitle on the cover that looked like some kind of self-help, that implied that something was wrong or broken with the reader (which is absolutely not true), that would also be a barrier.

Would you want to carry that book around with you? The one that screamed self-help and looked like a textbook? Would you want to leave it in your room in the open for someone to see if you weren't ready to tell them about it? We don't think so, and that's why we wanted to give you a book that you could feel good about having in your possession at any time. *FREEDOM* is yours, it's not a book for a broken person; *FREEDOM* is a book for any person. That's why the title is a single word and that's also why you will only find the subtitle on the title page inside the book.

We want to protect your privacy and give you something you will actually use and feel safe to carry around with you if you choose, without fear. We want you to feel free of judgement, ridicule or scorn whenever you see or pick up this book.

What Else Will You Notice that Might Seem Different?

As you begin to read and interact with this book, you will notice that some concepts are re-emphasized throughout all of the chapters. This is also on purpose. Some of these concepts and ideas are:

- ✧ We are all born with a TRICKY brain.
- ✧ Everyone struggles in life.
- ✧ It's not your fault that you have difficult thoughts and feelings—we all do.
- ✧ Mindfulness keeps the mind's attention in the here and now where life actually takes place.
- ✧ Your Compassionate Other and Compassionate Self are always there for you.
- ✧ We can use our compassionate mind skills and practices to help us soothe our minds and bodies. When we do this, we aren't trying to avoid difficult thoughts, emotions, or situations. Rather, we are learning to use compassionate mind skills to switch ourselves from a mind that is organized by threat into a more balanced state of mind. When we do this, it frees us up to be able to take action on what is truly important to us in life.

The more we integrate these ideas and practices into our lives the more helpful they are. The more you practice something the better you become at it. This is true for all things, even incorporating mindfulness and self-compassion into your everyday experiences.

Thriving in a Chaotic World and Growing a Purpose-driven Life

In order to thrive in this fast-paced, sometimes chaotic world, and grow a purpose-driven life, we need to be intentional and mindful in our thoughts, in our words, and in what we choose to do. Everyone struggles in this life, even if it doesn't seem like it at times. And during times of struggle, we can turn to compassionate practices to help us through these difficult situations and seasons. So even amidst the chaos, you can have a calm inner-knowing that you have the skills to handle the bumps in the road. And more than that, you have a foundation from which you can grow a purpose-driven life.

What exactly does it mean to grow a purpose-driven life? A purpose-driven life is built upon your values and the things that are truly important to you. When you are living life according to your values, you feel more content and fulfilled. This doesn't mean that you don't have hard times or bumps in the road, but in the face of these difficulties, you know that what you are doing is worth it. In a purpose-driven life, your actions are aligned with your values and the type of person you want to be—the highest version of yourself.

How to Use This Book

This book is meant to be a hands-on practical resource for you. This is your book to do with as you wish. It's a book that you can come back to again and again. As you can see, the book is separated into two parts. Part 1: The Untold Story, is the background on why we think the way we do and also why we do the things we do. We hope it will give you some knowledge and understanding but also give you hope and the opportunity to release any shame around the difficult thoughts and emotions you may experience. We do recommend that the first time you read and interact with this book you start at the beginning, reading and completing the reflections in Part 1 (Chapters 1-3) before moving on to the practices. Part 1 will give you a great foundation for understanding before moving into the compassionate mind practices and skills in Part 2 (Chapters 4-9).

Part 2: The Practices, is a collection of 33 practices to help you navigate the difficult emotions and thoughts that may come up as you are living boldly according to your values and your purpose-driven life. We realize that 33 practices may seem like a lot. Think about them like a buffet. You don't have to eat everything on the buffet in one sitting. You can sample the ones that look good to you and then come back again and again to try others. And unlike a food buffet, these practices will never go bad and never run out, so go slow if that feels good to you. Use the practices that resonate with you and then try something new when you feel ready.

You will notice that there are lots of opportunities to interact with this book and its practices. This is on purpose, too. We wholeheartedly encourage you to write, draw, and doodle your way through the book, making it your own. You will also notice at the ends of the chapters and at the end of the book we have left space for you to further make this book your own. Use this space for whatever you like: doodles, drawings, reflections, or just pure nonsense! Have fun with it!

Since some of these practices are such that it would be helpful to have them as guided practices, we have also included audio versions of these on our website for the book (www.MindfulCompssionForTeens.com). We encourage you to listen to the guided meditation practices when you first try them out. Having an audio recording to guide you can be very helpful when first learning mindfulness and compassion skills. Please use these resources as often as you like to help you on your journey! The more you practice these skills the more they will start naturally showing up for you when you need them the most in your daily life. And while this book is for teens—for you—you should know that we use many of these same practices with our adult clients and with ourselves. These practices work over time and can be a comfort to you for your whole life.

The Art in This Book

The art in this book is very special. As we were writing this book, we constantly envisioned a design and art for the book that would bring our content to life and also reinforce the message of mindful compassion at every turn of the page. To do this we enlisted two amazing artists: Heather Preston and Stephen Swartz.

Heather Preston's art pieces are the nature-inspired illustrations you see featured on the front cover as well as the beginning of each chapter and the end of most of the chapters. Heather Preston is Chris's aunt and she is a highly celebrated and award-winning artist, book illustrator, and commercial illustrator. What is not so well known about Heather Preston is that like Chris she struggled with dyslexia as a teenager and still does as an adult. The art featured in this book is inspired by the healing power of nature and connectedness.

Nature is so calming, inspiring, and rejuvenating. In fact, recent research at the University of Michigan has shown that just 20 minutes out in nature reduces stress and creates a greater sense of well-being (Hunter, Gillespie & Chen, 2019). Sometimes, though, you don't have access or can't get outside. If you find you can't venture out into nature, we think these illustrations will bring nature to you in some small way. We invite you to linger over these illustrations; we know each time you look at these pieces you will see some new discovery and we hope you will feel the intention of comfort and love coming off of the page.

Stephen Swartz's art pieces are the hand illustrations that you see featured with each reflection and practice in the book. These represent the comfort of your Compassionate Other and your Compassionate Self. So when you see these images, we would like you to remember that you are never alone. You are always cared for. You are always enough just as you are (even if your mind tells you otherwise).

We hope this book brings you a sense of comfort, safeness, and courage in a world filled with chaos. We hope as you read and use the practices in the book you will also feel empowered to boldly live your purpose-driven life.

"Still round the corner there may wait

A new road or a secret gate

And though I oft have passed them by

A day will come at last when I

Shall take the hidden paths that run

West of the Moon, East of the Sun."

J.R.R. Tolkien

Dedication

For Eva

For all of us

"Keep climbing that mountain, keep looking up, and in the stillness of your thoughts you will find comfort and the will to carry on."

Bobby Fraser

Chris's grandfather, who fought for Scotland in the First World War, inscribed this in a book for Chris in 1981 and now we inscribe it here for you…

Part One

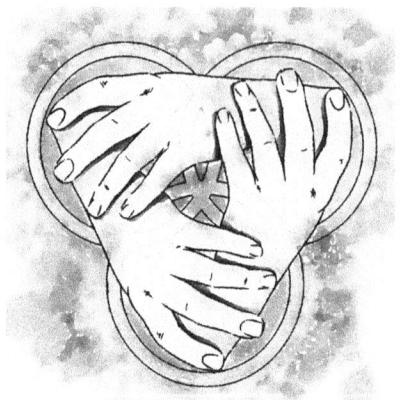

The Untold Story

CHAPTER 1: We Are All Connected

CHAPTER 2: It's Not Your Fault

CHAPTER 3: You Are Not Alone

We Are All Connected

"We are all affecting the world every moment, whether we mean to or not. Our actions and states of mind matter, because we are so deeply interconnected with one another."

Ram Dass

Welcome!
We are so glad you've found this book.

For many of us, the idea that we are all connected is a tough one to wrap our minds around. Often it doesn't feel like we are connected, especially when we are hurting and feeling alone.

You are not alone, though. Throughout this book we will share lots of information, but one of the biggest takeaways is this message that we are not alone. It's really important.

But why would you listen to what we have to say?

Most people need to feel a connection with someone in order to trust them. We need to know that they have experienced challenges too, that they understand on some level where we are coming from.

So, we would like to share a bit about our stories and why we are writing this book in the first place. And just maybe you'll find something that you can relate to in your own experience.

We are asking you to take a chance on us. And, if you still aren't interested in what we have to say, you never have to pick up this book again.

Chris's Story

Here's the deal: I was a teen who had chronic acne. I was also very skinny with slouched shoulders. So now you are beginning to form a mental picture of me, but it's still not the whole story.

I also had ADHD, dyslexia, and learning disabilities. I would try not to be noticed in the classroom because I often did not understand what was going on and I did not want anyone to discover how lost I was. My acne was so bad that I tried not to look people in the eyes because I didn't want them to see my face. I really just wanted to hide all day long.

I felt stressed and scared at school because with ADHD I was often losing things and was chronically disorganized. I would never ask questions in class. I did not want my peers to think I was stupid because I didn't understand the work.

I was scared to ask girls out because I thought they would be disgusted by my severe acne. I would avoid looking in mirrors because I didn't want to see my face full of zits. If I did look in a mirror it was from a distance so I wouldn't be able to see the details of my crater face.

I still remember sitting in the back seat of my parent's car, seeing my reflection in the side mirror and having the thought, "I hate myself."

I would pretend I was sick all the time and even would come up with elaborate schemes to get out of school. One of my more creative schemes involved hiding cans of cream of mushroom soup in the cabinet under the bathroom sink. In the middle of the night, I would open a can and splatter it in the toilet to make it look like I had been sick. I would then bring my blankets and pillow into the bathroom and sleep there the rest of the night. In the morning my mom would find me there and I would put on my sick act and she would have mercy on me.

I felt stupid and ugly most of the time and wanted to be any place but school. I would even miss the bus on purpose and hide in the woods behind my house. I would then sneak back in after my parents went to work. My dad caught me once and the result wasn't pretty. He tried to lay down the law with me. He just kept saying,

"You have to go to school. It's not up for discussion."

As you can imagine, that didn't sit well with me. One thing led to another and in my anger and sadness, I blurted out "#%&@ YOU! And as you can also imagine that didn't sit well with him! He chased me out the back door and tackled me in the backyard. He pinned me to the ground, we were both crying, and needless to say I went begrudgingly to school that day.

I was hurting inside so badly, but it seemed like nobody knew or cared.

I had a good friend who also struggled with ADHD and dyslexia and we consoled each other, but he went to a different school. So most of the time I still felt like I was alone, even though I knew that my best friend understood what I was going through.

I failed classes in school and had to go to summer school, mostly due to the numerous missing homework assignments that would regularly bring down my grades. I would try to do my homework, but I just didn't seem to understand most of the time. Of course, because I didn't understand, I ultimately just felt stupid and would avoid doing my work. My solution of avoidance also involved telling my parents and teachers lies to get them off my back.

I wanted to do well, but I was just so sad and demoralized. And really, as I look back now, I just didn't know what to do. I would get frustrated easily with my parents and I would often be mean to my younger sister who I was jealous of because she didn't have my challenges.

I felt like I had to keep all this inner struggle a secret so no one would see how inadequate and stupid I was. I didn't have the skills, strategies, or the understanding that would have made a big difference.

The one place where I did feel better about myself was on the soccer field. I was a good player, but definitely not the best player. I loved being outside running free on the soccer field.

You see, on the field, I could escape that punishing voice in my head telling me over and over again that I wasn't good enough. On the field, I was in the present moment with my teammates who valued me.

Heather's Story

My experience was very different than Chris's and yet I still felt like I was never enough. Or sometimes I was too much. Whatever I felt I was, it just wasn't right. I excelled in the academics of school, but I struggled socially and developed a very shrewd and busy inner critic. Perfectionism ruled my life. Anything less than perfect wasn't good enough, including myself. And since we humans are imperfect beings, that meant that I wasn't enough— ever.

I had a life that was fairly sheltered. I followed all of the rules. In fact, the rules really ran my life. I studied hard and was rewarded for this by having a nearly perfect report card every year. I was dependable and responsible.

Everything looked perfect from the outside and that's what kept me trapped.

I struggled with my weight and at a fairly young age was put on a diet by our family doctor. When I look back on this now, I know it was completely appropriate for me to be the weight I was at the time—right before hitting puberty—but I was devastated.

The prescription was not to cut anything out exactly, but to just eat half of what I ate every day. Half. So breakfast became a half bowl of cereal or a half piece of toast, and lunch was half a sandwich and half an apple. I remember eating that lunch from fifth grade all the way through high school. And it was a constant reminder that I couldn't be trusted with food.

Food was a place of shame and guilt. Even if I followed all the "rules" my body would betray me by being hungry. I lost the required weight but stayed on the program (most of the time) because those were the rules. And if I didn't follow them I would end up in the place where I started, disappointing my parents and myself.

Our family moved when I was entering eighth grade and I went from a 250-student school to a 1200-student school in a different state eight hours away. This essentially amounted to culture shock for me. I hid myself away. I retreated into my books and to food. I gained weight. I had trouble making friends for a couple of years. I felt depressed and sad. I ate when I was feeling hurt. I ate as a reward. I ate to fill up a void that just couldn't be filled. I'm sure I was also angry, but that wasn't an emotion that I felt comfortable with, so I retreated deeper into myself.

Again, I was doing great with the academics of school, but I dreaded any social time—lunch or anything that was essentially "free" time. I received praise for being smart and musically talented, so I spent all my time there. And that was really quite wonderful at times.

> I lost myself in books and writing and singing. But ask me a question that wasn't related to things where I excelled and I would become almost paralyzed.

I would run through conversations in my head over and over again. In my mind, everything I said out loud never seemed to come out right. I was constantly on guard with what I said to people because I didn't want to say the "wrong" thing. Consequently, I didn't say very much. This did teach me how to observe though—people, relationships, situations, patterns, beauty, everything really.

My perfectionism had another side too. I rarely ventured out into trying new things because I understood that when you try something new, you aren't going to be good at it. You aren't going to be perfect at something that is new. So I avoided anything that looked like a risk.

I felt very alone. My inner critic was always on high alert telling me I was fat and ugly, smart and really nice—but no one really likes "nice girls" do they? It didn't feel like it to me at that time in my life.

It's Not Your Fault

Although we have made peace with these things and they have shaped who we are and how we live our lives in a positive way, we wish we could go back in time. If we could time travel to the past, we would comfort and support our teenage selves who were hurting so deeply. We would share with them the information and the practices in this book that could have helped to ease some of the internal struggle. Above all else, we would tell our teenage selves:

It's Not Your Fault!

No one chooses to be born with ADHD, or to learn that anything less than perfect isn't good enough. Like these younger versions of ourselves didn't choose to experience these challenges, we know that if you are struggling with something, you didn't choose your struggles either. Even though we cannot physically go back to those pivotal points in our lives, we can comfort those teenage versions of ourselves that experienced this pain and still show up occasionally in our adult lives. And we can be here for you now. We can support you.

Our motivation to write this book comes from our own inner struggles as teenagers. We didn't have a lot of self-compassion and we want to give you the tools that we wish we had when we were growing up. We hope that the compassionate wisdom and information in this book will help set you free and as a result, you will pursue things that are important to you!

REFLECTION:

What was it like for you to read our stories? What showed up in your mind?

When you think about your own story or life, do you see any similarities or differences to what we have shared about our experiences?

Why Compassion?

When we talk about compassion in this book we have a very specific and clear definition:

"Compassion is a sensitivity to suffering in oneself and others with a commitment to try to alleviate and prevent it."

Dr. Paul Gilbert, Founder of
Compassion Focused Therapy (CFT)

Bringing compassion into your life (self-compassion) and showing compassion to others takes courage and wisdom. We have to be willing to turn towards our own suffering and the suffering of others, even when we feel like we want to run away from it or avoid it at all costs. In turning towards the suffering we are able to see our common humanity—at certain times in our lives, all of us struggle and suffer. It's not a constant, but it is part of this journey of life that we all travel.

First though, we would like to invite you to come along on a journey with us. In Chapter 2: It's Not Our Fault we are going to dive right in. We want to give you insight into why we struggle with our "tricky" brains, and how we might understand our reactions and responses to the difficulties we all face—our common humanity. This wisdom gives us the choice and the freedom to have a different response in the face of these struggles.

The Important Stuff

✧ You are not alone. We are all connected in a common humanity.

✧ The way you are feeling is not your fault.

✧ We want to give you the tools that we wish we had when we were growing up. We hope that the compassionate wisdom and information in this book will help set you free and as a result, you will pursue things that are important to you!

For more resources, guided practices, and meditations, please visit our website: www.MindfulCompassionForTeens.com.

"Our human compassion binds
us the one to the other—not
in pity or patronisingly, but
as human beings who have
learnt how to turn our common
suffering into hope for the
future."

Nelson Mandela

It's Not Our Fault

"Every person has their secret sorrows which the world knows not..."

Henry Wadsworth Longfellow

Everyone Struggles

It doesn't always seem like it, but everyone struggles at one time or another.

Even people who look like they have it all together experience difficult times.

The tough part about being human is that when we make mistakes our brains hit us with strong emotions and thoughts. These thoughts start to attack us in an attempt to fix the mistake or problem. You see, our brains have a really important job—to keep us safe.

This response of attacking ourselves is a refrain that is meant to keep us "safe," but in reality it isn't safe at all.

The refrain sounds something like this:

You're not good enough.

How could you do something so stupid?

You can never get it right, can you? And on and on and on.

Our minds often tell us that it's all our fault! Can you hear the tone of that voice in your head—even right now? We all have that voice in our heads.

These harsh thoughts come on so fast and so often that we don't ever realize that we could have a different experience.

So why does this happen?

Let's start with the source—our brains. It's not our fault that we were born with the brain we have. We don't have any choice about what we are given when we are born. We don't have any choice about the brain we have. We didn't have the opportunity to design it before we were born. We just found ourselves with it. On top of that, our brain changes more during our teenage years than at any other time of life except for when we were toddlers. All of these massive changes can make a challenging time of life even more challenging.

> And just so we are on the same page, we want to be really clear about something before we go any further—as our friend Dr. Paul Gilbert (the founder of Compassion Focused Therapy) says, our brain is TRICKY.

But here's the thing—through understanding how our tricky brain works we can find more freedom in our lives. This might sound crazy, but stay with us.

When we understand how our brain works we realize that there are good reasons for why it works the way it does. We would guess that you haven't been exposed to all of these details—we weren't. This new knowledge helps us understand why we feel what we feel and also why we do what we do.

The Untold Story

Our brain is divided into two basic parts: the old brain and the new brain, and we didn't always have both parts. The brain we have today is a result of millions of years of evolution.

That's right, evolution! Don't worry, we're not going hard-core science here. We just want to share with you why our brain works the way it does.

Our brain has evolved to keep us alive and its purpose is to keep us safe above all else. This idea that our brains have evolved over time means that not a single one of us were able to customize our brain like we would customize a new computer with all the features we desire. We have no choice whatsoever in the brain we are given. Our friend Dr. Paul Gilbert talks about the old brain and the new brain in his books and how these different parts of our brain show up and impact everything we do in life (Gilbert, 2010; 2014).

The Old Brain

The old brain evolved to help our ancestors survive and keep them safe. We share this old brain with our pets and animals. This part of our brain—our old brain—evolved around 500 million years ago!

Sometimes this old brain is referred to as the reptilian brain. You won't be surprised to find out that the reptilian brain developed with the evolution of reptiles. This part of the brain helps us to navigate dangers, to develop basic defensive behaviors, to pursue resources, and to help facilitate the survival of our species (Gilbert, 2010; 2014). This part of our brain starts changing when we are around eleven or twelve and is pretty much fully developed by the time we are fifteen or sixteen.

After the evolution of the reptilian brain, the mammalian brain (mammals emerged about 200 million years ago) continued to add to the old brain functions. So where we had the emotions of fear, anger, desire, and lust, now, with the mammalian brain we added to these emotions bonding, play, joy, and sadness (Gilbert, 2010; 2014).

As you can see, the old brain is key to our survival and also motivates us to be competitive (competing for food, shelter, partners) and to show caregiving to those around us. No one could survive alone for long in prehistoric times so the need to provide caregiving, like a mother would to a child, was essential for survival.

Let's stop and think about this for a second. The people who had the strongest and most well-developed competitive and caregiving motivations survived beyond those who did not. These people then had children and passed these traits on to the next generation. So as you can see, these traits served a very important life-or-death purpose on more than one level.

The way our brains developed was not a planned out or engineered process. Our brains were shaped by a rather random process of adaptive evolution—meaning humans have developed traits that have ensured our survival—over thousands of years. This is the reason we are here on earth at this very moment.

The New Brain

Now for the new brain! The new brain evolved much later, around two million years ago. (That's not what we normally think of as "new" but two million years is new in evolutionary terms!) This new brain can problem solve and has the ability to imagine, think, plan, organize, juggle multiple ideas and tasks, and remember instructions. This part of your brain starts changing around the same time as the old brain but is not finished developing until much later. Your new brain doesn't finish developing until you are in your mid-twenties. In the book *Brainstorm: The Power and Purpose of the Teenage Brain*, Dr. Dan Siegel talks about how these brain changes are actually preparing us to meet the challenges of the adult world.

The new brain is capable of complex thinking abilities linked to the part of our brain called the prefrontal cortex. This part of the brain allows us to imagine things and create images in our mind. These images may be real (from our own life) or they could be completely made up. These images can both help us and also sometimes cause us pain, discomfort, stress, or anxiety.

Other abilities of our new brain include being able to puzzle through social relationships, predict and consider possible future outcomes in our lives, plan for events or goals we want to accomplish or achieve, and even reflect upon the past (Gilbert, 2010; 2014).

Sometimes these reflection and prediction capabilities can cause us to struggle, though. We may dwell on mistakes that happened in the past or predict worst-case scenarios in the future and because our brains have evolved to do this, it's not our fault that we do have these struggles. With all of these abilities and functions, though, our brain has one common purpose—keeping us safe at all costs.

With these new-brain abilities, artists can create amazing works of art, songwriters and storytellers can put together words on a page that can bring you to emotional highs and lows, engineers and doctors can create and utilize science and technology that changes our lives, and the list could go on and on.

Our pets and animals don't have these abilities.

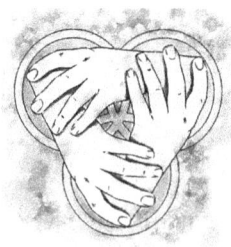

REFLECTION:

After reading about the old brain and the new brain, what thoughts or feelings show up for you?

When we say it's not our fault that we have this tricky brain, what does that mean to you?

We are asking you these reflection questions to begin inviting the practice of mindfulness. According to Dr. Jon Kabat-Zinn, who is known for bringing mindfulness to mainstream society, "Mindfulness means paying attention in a particular way: on purpose, in the present moment, and nonjudgmentally" (Kabat-Zinn 1994). Mindfulness is a way to purposely build our ability to pay attention to what is happening on the inside (in our minds and in our bodies) and also what is happening on the outside (around us). Noticing what is happening inside us and around us in an open and curious way, without judgement, helps us to bring our attention back to the present moment so we can do the things that are important to us.

Old and New Brain Interactions—Loops

To see how we share this old brain with animals and how much tougher it is to be a human with new-brain capabilities, let's look at something that many people can relate to: our pets. Our friend Dr. Russell Kolts talks about his dog in his book *CFT Made Simple* and how the old brain shows up in animals. This made us start thinking about our dog Coco and how she behaves on a daily basis. Coco is a little 14-pound white dog who loves to take naps in the sun in front of the sliding glass doors in our house.

Occasionally a small neighborhood dog named Chucky finds his way into our backyard and then pees right in front of the glass doors where Coco likes to sleep. You should know that Chucky is a Yorkshire Terrier (weighing less than 10 pounds) who bit Coco on the nose when she was a puppy.

When Chucky shows up and pees in our yard in front of Coco's face, her old brain kicks in. Coco gets angry and barks like crazy until Chucky leaves. All her energy and motivation is focused on protecting her property (and people) from Chucky. Once Chucky leaves, Coco resumes her nap in the sun relatively quickly.

However, things are much different when the big Doberman Pinscher named McLovin gets loose and finds his way into our backyard. Coco's threat system becomes activated just as it does when Chucky is around, but instead of barking like crazy, she gets low to the ground and growls menacingly, but softly. It's as if she is saying,

"Get out of here McLovin, but please, please don't eat me!"

McLovin eventually leaves and Coco again goes back to sleeping peacefully in the sun like nothing ever happened.

The new brain on the other hand is something that Coco does not have. So let's try an experiment with our new brain's ability to imagine things. Let's imagine what it might be like if we found ourselves in a similar situation as our dog Coco.

Imagine yourself going to bed tonight and in the middle of the night you hear a strange noise. You jump out of bed and to your surprise you discover a very small 11-year-old kid with no weapon trying to break into your house and steal all your electronics!

There is a very good chance that you would feel angry, and like my dog Coco, you would scream until the child left. You might even chase them off of your property. (Coco would certainly do that if she was outside when Chucky appeared.)

Now let's try to imagine the same situation, but this time when you hear something strange at night you discover that there is large man with a gun trying to break into your house and steal your electronics. In this circumstance you would most likely feel very scared and like Coco you might lay low—quietly calling the police. You wouldn't want this intruder in your house, but you also wouldn't want to draw too much attention to yourself and put yourself in more danger.

However, unlike Coco our new brain would probably make it very difficult for us to go back to sleep after the intruder leaves. Our new brain would have all kinds of scary images and thoughts. Thoughts like,

"What if the intruder comes back? Maybe he's still here hiding somewhere around the house. What if he shot me?"

And many other fearful thoughts.

It's not only that we would have these thoughts, though. Because we have both the new-brain and old-brain capabilities, both come into play. Our new-brain thoughts and images of possible scary outcomes would then loop down to the old brain and wake up real fear and anger even after the actual danger has passed.

This fear, anger, and anxiety would then send a message back up to the new brain, "YOU ARE IN DANGER!" And this message, then, would create even more fearful images and thoughts. Loops.

The result is us lying in bed awake with this loop of new-brain thoughts and images triggering old brain feelings and emotions over and over. In fact, the longer these loops go on, the more we may begin to attack ourselves with thoughts like,

"Why didn't I wake someone up first? Why didn't I call the police immediately? I can never do anything right."

The Loops in Our Heads

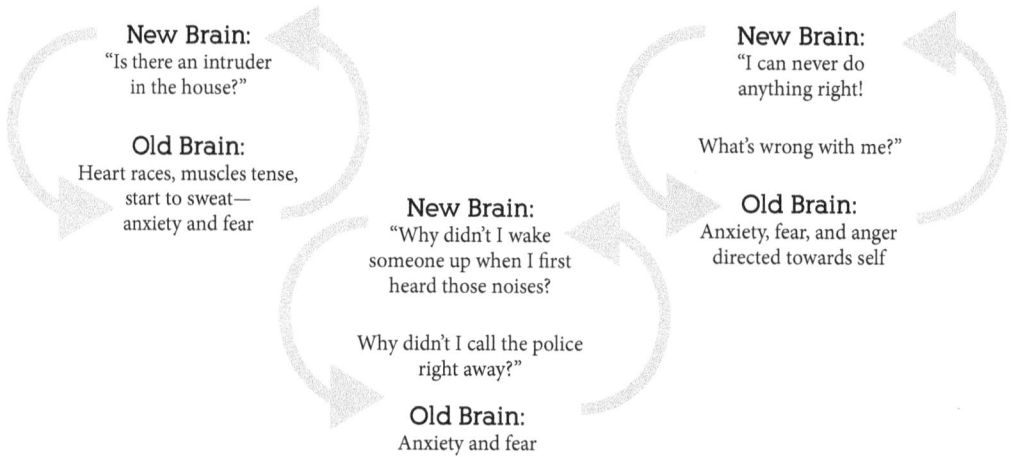

New Brain:
"Is there an intruder
in the house?"

Old Brain:
Heart races, muscles tense,
start to sweat—
anxiety and fear

New Brain:
"Why didn't I wake
someone up when I first
heard those noises?

Why didn't I call the police
right away?"

Old Brain:
Anxiety and fear

New Brain:
"I can never do
anything right!

What's wrong with me?"

Old Brain:
Anxiety, fear, and anger
directed towards self

This would create an almost continuous loop over and over again, like a dog chasing its own tail. Even if the police were to call us almost immediately and tell us that they caught the intruder we would still most likely not be able to sleep soundly because of this tricky new-brain and old-brain merry-go-round.

You see, our new brain gives us the ability to trigger ourselves over and over with recurring images or new images that are even more traumatizing than the actual event that occurred in real life (Irons, 2018). Our ability to imagine, predict, and anticipate goes into overdrive, creating scenarios that leave us activating even more of our old brain emotions of anxiety, fear, anger, and disgust. All of this looping is designed to—you guessed it—keep us safe, but it isn't really doing that any more. Instead it is keeping us stuck with our attention hyper-focused on the threat in front of us (Gilbert, 2010; 2014).

On the other hand, if we look back at our dog Coco we would find her sleeping soundly without a care in the world. Living in the world today with both the old brain and this evolved new brain of ours is challenging, and it's not our fault that we get caught up in these looping cycles.

The Three Circles of Emotion

Now that we understand a little bit more about this tricky evolved brain of ours we can look deeper and discover a couple more secrets that we were never told.

We have inherited three basic emotional systems to help us stay alive and keep us safe:

Threat—Drive—Soothe.

All three of these systems have helped humans stay alive and none of us would be here today if our ancestors didn't have them. Again, just like the old brain and the new brain, no one was able to choose or design these emotional systems. These systems organize our brains and create the experiences we have in the world (Gilbert, 2009).

So what does that mean when we say that these systems organize our brains and create the experiences we have in the world? Have you noticed that when you are feeling different emotions such as happiness, anger, peacefulness, fear, or sadness that you behave differently and respond differently to what is going on around you?

It's almost as if a different version of you shows up depending on the emotions you are feeling.

For example, if you are upset about a grade you received in third period you most likely won't feel like joking or chatting with a friend about what happened at lunch. But, if you had a great day and everything seemed to go just right, you would be more likely to smile, be nicer to your younger sibling, or answer the questions your parents ask you about your day with more patience and ease.

It's sort of like trying on different pairs of prescription glasses. When you look through one pair of glasses the world looks one way, and when you try on a different pair the same world looks very different. So different emotions affect our mind and bodies in very different ways. Each emotional system Threat, Drive, or Soothe has a very different effect on where our attention goes, the way we think about things, the mental imagery we have in our minds, and the general emotional experience we feel. When we become more mindfully aware of these systems in our lives it is easier to see how they influence our thinking, feeling, attention, behaviors and how we respond to what is going on around us (Gilbert, 2009; Gilbert & Choden, 2014).

How the Three Emotional Systems Organize Our Minds

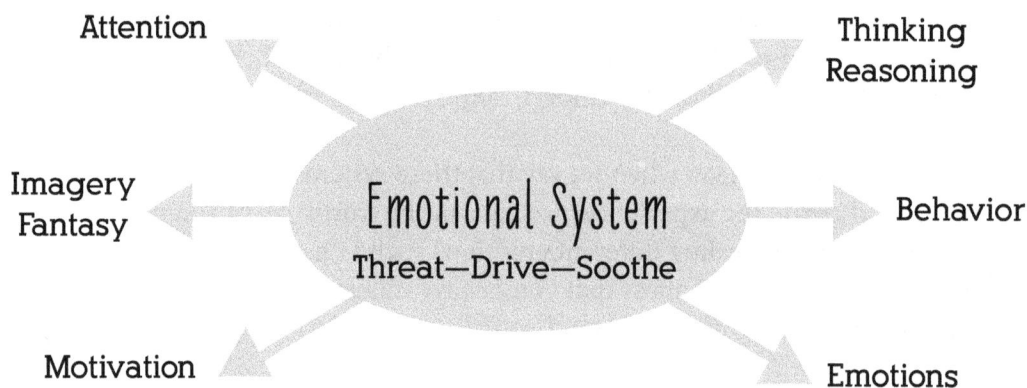

Attention

Thinking
Reasoning

Imagery
Fantasy

Emotional System
Threat—Drive—Soothe

Behavior

Motivation

Emotions

Threat System

The Threat "protection" System keeps us on the lookout for possible dangers that could harm us or the people we care about. This system is designed to keep us safe at all costs.

> The Threat System is like an alarm system that activates our defensive emotions and influences our behavior to fight, run away (flight), or freeze.

Some of the emotions we think of when we are in our Threat System are anger, anxiety, and disgust. The behaviors that often go along with these Threat System emotions are aggression, avoidance, and submission (Gilbert, 2009).

As you can see, both the emotions and behaviors that are part of the Threat System aren't pleasant or comfortable. In fact, they can cause a lot of distress and pain, but that doesn't mean that the Threat System is all bad. This system serves a very real purpose for us and for our primitive ancestors. This system has evolved over time to keep us safe and protect us from danger and motivate us to take action when we need to. When we are in the Threat System, our attention is hyper-focused or very narrowly focused on whatever we perceive the threat to be in that moment. All of our attention and thinking is organized by the threat we perceive and it is very difficult to concentrate on anything else (Kolts, 2016).

Let's look at an emotion that you might not think about all of the time—disgust. Now, if you are looking at this from the Threat System perspective you are feeling disgust for a very specific reason. Maybe you start to eat something and it is rotten—it's truly disgusting! So, you don't swallow it; you immediately spit it out and rinse your mouth out with water. Or maybe you volunteer to help cook dinner and you take the chicken out of the refrigerator and unwrap it, only to be nearly suffocated by a terrible smell. Instead of cooking it you dump it out, knowing that it would make you and your family sick.

Disgust can be attributed to a person or a situation too. When we feel disgusted in the presence of a person or during a situation that goes against our beliefs and values, we usually try to leave as quickly as possible. Or if we can't leave at that moment we certainly don't go looking for that experience again. The person or the situation is toxic so your Threat System tells you to get out and don't come back!

> When the Threat System is activated your body jumps into high gear, and all you can focus on or think about is that threat. This enables you to take action—fight, flee, or freeze—whatever you need most in that particular situation.

Drive System

The second system is the Drive "excitement" System. This system is also known as the resource-seeking system. This system motivates us to pursue the important things that we need in order to survive in this life: food, shelter, or a partner.

This system is active, exciting, and competitive. In fact, when we are actively searching for these life basics we experience a thrill that is enticing, rewarding, and pleasurable. This is the system that creates an urgency in us to pursue the things we need to survive and things that are meaningful to us (Gilbert, 2009).

When we are in our Drive System our attention and thinking is focused on the goal in front of us (Kolts, 2016). We may feel emotions like excitement, joy or anticipation. These emotions activate behaviors to move towards those things we want in our lives and our goals too. Once we achieve some of those things, our feelings of excitement and joy then reinforce our actions and in turn motivate us to do more in the future.

You may be thinking right about now that the Drive System is totally awesome and we should stay in high drive all of the time. But similar to how the Threat System isn't all bad, the Drive System isn't all good. If we stay in our Drive System too much or too often without a break—without a balance from our Soothe System—we can burn out. What once was a positive turns into a negative because we have no more internal resources to continue in our drive towards the things that are important to us and that we need to survive.

Soothe System

The third system is the Soothing System, which could be described as the noncompetitive, chill out, rest, and digest system. This system allows us to recharge, by creating the positive feelings of well-being, contentment, warmth, nurturance, and peacefulness (Gilbert, 2009). When we are in our Soothe System, our attention and focus is open and reflective and we experience a sense of safeness and calm (Kolts, 2016).

As you may have guessed from our discussions on the Threat and Drive systems—although we need these systems for survival, we can't stay in these two systems all of the time. If we are constantly on the move pursuing our dreams, goals or other important things in our life (food, shelter, partner) or if we are always under attack or anticipating threat we will soon become burned out and exhausted.

> We all need to give ourselves time to relax and recover. The ability to take the time we need to rest and give ourselves much needed self-care is truly important. If we don't purposely and intentionally take this time, the Threat and Drive systems will take over.

The Soothing System is not just the absence of Threat and Drive. Like the Threat and Drive systems, though, the Soothe System reinforces our emotions of contentment, calmness, and peacefulness. And as you have probably guessed by now, we can't hang out in the Soothe System forever either. We need our Drive and Threat systems, otherwise we would just be eating pizza and binging Netflix 24/7.

These systems have worked together historically to help humans stay alive, and none of us would be here today if our ancestors didn't have them. Each system Threat, Drive, Soothe influences how we see the world and our experience in the world. Whatever system we are in at the moment directs our thinking and reasoning, attention, imagery, motivation, emotions, and our behavior. Ideally they all work in a balanced way, but sometimes—in fact more often than not—our three systems can become unbalanced.

What we are really trying to achieve is a balance of the three systems.

A Balancing Act: Using Compassion

Remember when we talked about the evolution of the mammalian brain and its ability and need to give and receive bonding, affection, care, and kindness from others? At that point, evolution began to shape the Soothing System to be highly sensitive to these signals of kindness, care, and affection. Mammals, including humans, need to be held, cared for, cuddled, etc., in order to thrive.

And also remember from Chapter 1 our definition of compassion:

"Compassion is a sensitivity to suffering in oneself and others with a commitment to try to alleviate and prevent it."

Dr. Paul Gilbert

Compassionate responses help us to activate our Soothing System when we need it most (through the many different practices that we explore throughout this book). In activating our Soothing System, we are able to choose to slow down before taking action—take a mindful pause—to turn towards the people around us to gain a sense of safeness and support, and to downshift our Threat System.

We can use these compassionate practices to help us mindfully tolerate distress and meet challenges when they arise. Compassionate mind training allows us to create a space for openness and balance in our brain and feel more clear and flexible in our thought processes and actions.

The Important Stuff

✧ Everyone struggles at one time or another even if it doesn't seem like it. We all have a tricky brain that evolved over millions of years to keep us safe at all costs. Our brain is made up of two basic parts—the old brain and the new brain.

✧ The old brain is key to our survival and also motivates us to be competitive and to show caregiving to those around us. The new brain can problem-solve and has the ability to imagine, think, plan, organize, juggle multiple ideas and tasks, and remember instructions. Other abilities of our new brain include being able to puzzle through social relationships, predict and consider possible future outcomes in our lives, plan for events or goals we want to accomplish or achieve, and even reflect upon the past.

✧ Our old brain and new brain often get caught in loops like a dog chasing its tail. A difficult event happens that creates a threat in our lives. Our old-brain emotions of anxiety, fear, and anger are triggered. Our new-brain abilities to imagine, predict, and anticipate go into overdrive and create images that are sometimes even more traumatizing than the actual events that occurred in real life. All of this looping is designed to keep us safe, but instead it keeps us stuck.

✧ We have inherited three basic emotional systems to help us stay alive and keep us safe: Threat—Drive—Soothe.

- The Threat System has evolved over time protect us from danger and motivate us to take action when we need to. The Threat System activates our defensive emotions that influence our behavior to fight, run away, or freeze. Emotions that show up include anger, anxiety, and disgust, and the behaviors that often go along with these emotions are aggression, avoidance, and submission.

- The Drive System motivates us to pursue the important things that we need in order to survive: food, shelter, or a partner. This system is active, exciting, and competitive. When we are searching for these life basics we experience a thrill that is enticing, rewarding, and pleasurable, and we may feel emotions like excitement, joy or anticipation.

- The Soothe System allows us to recharge by creating the positive feelings of well-being, contentment, warmth, nurturance, and peacefulness. If we don't purposely and intentionally take this time to soothe, the Threat and Drive systems will take over.

- Compassionate mindful responses help us to activate our Soothing System when we need it most. In activating our Soothing System, we are able to choose to slow down before taking action, to turn towards the people around us to gain a sense of safeness and support, and to downshift our Threat System. We can use these compassionate mindful practices to help us tolerate distress and meet challenges when they arise.

For more resources, guided practices, and meditations, please visit our website:
www.MindfulCompassionForTeens.com.

It's Not Our Fault   -34-

"So much of what we are then has been completely outside of our control and is not our fault."

Paul Gilbert

It's Not Our Fault

You Are Not Alone

"Whatever my individual desires were to be free, I was not alone. There were many others who felt the same way."

Rosa Parks

Sometimes we all need alone time. In fact, sometimes it feels good to go off by ourselves and just be alone. But, as humans, we are the most social species on the planet and therefore none of us truly wants to be alone forever. In fact, it gives us comfort and strength, and helps to activate our Soothing System, to know that we are not alone. There is an old saying from Lao Tzu (an ancient Chinese philosopher) that says,

"Being deeply loved gives you strength while loving someone deeply gives you courage."

You may be wondering what this has to do with anything. The major reason we spent all that time talking about our brain and emotions in Chapter 2 was to help us understand that we are truly not alone. Each and every one of us starts out with a brain that has evolved to keep us safe. Each of us has this tricky brain that creates struggles in our lives, but we all want to be loved and accepted just as we are. So why do we feel so alone sometimes even when we are surrounded by others?

Myth #1

In order to have a good life you must be happy, confident, calm, and content all of the time.

We live in a culture in which people pretend they are happy, confident, calm, and content all of the time. Just think about spending an entire day interacting with people and how many times you would be asked,

"How are you today?" Most of us simply respond with something like, "Good. How are you?" or "Fine, thanks." or, "Not bad."

You have probably never heard someone respond—let's say a random person we come into contact with at the grocery store—

"I feel really depressed and I'm having thoughts of dying. How are you today?"

In fact, we are so conditioned to this automatic response of "fine" that we often just give that response to everyone, even to the people that we feel most connected to, like family and friends.

The fact that everyone is pretending to be happy all the time makes us feel that we are alone with our struggles, when actually we are not. It is so very rare to see friends on social media posting about how miserable, anxious, sad, and scared they are. Instead we see pictures and posts of people having the times of their lives at parties, on vacation, or doing other cool stuff with big smiles on their faces. This all feeds into our sense of thinking that we are alone with our difficulties, struggles, and pain.

This social comparison is just what our brain has evolved to do to help keep us safe. Our primitive survival instinct asks us over and over again,

"Am I fitting in? Am I contributing enough? Am I doing anything that might get me thrown out of the tribe?"

We all find ourselves doing this and it's not our fault. It is just what our mind has evolved to do. It has evolved to keep us safe which means not getting kicked out of our community.

In some ways, modern-day life is even harder than ancient times because we no longer live in small groups. We live in enormous groups! The fact that we have phones that expose us to thousands of images and stories of people all over the planet ramps up our social comparison even more because now we are comparing ourselves to thousands of people rather than just a few, like our primitive ancestors.

Today's society sends us messages all of the time—some of them are obvious, but many of them are not so obvious. These messages tell us that if we are not happy then something is wrong with us. If people were to learn how to be willing and open about the fact that they struggle with self-critical thoughts and difficult emotions, we would see that everyone struggles. We would see that struggling with self-critical thoughts, tough emotions, and difficult life circumstances is just part of life because each one of us has this evolved mind that can be very tricky.

It's good to take a moment to note that the evolutionary reason why people don't actually open up about their inner critical thoughts and difficult emotions is that people don't want to be seen as inadequate.

People instinctively fear that if they are seen as inadequate or unworthy then they may be rejected by those around them. Today, rejection isn't the end of the world because we do live in such large groups and have access to many different opportunities to create relationships (sometimes even outside of our immediate geographic area) but a long time ago, rejection could have even meant death. As we have evolved, this basic instinct to remain connected to the group at all costs has stayed with us.

You are not alone.

Myth #2

You are weak if you feel sad when you are alone.

We all hurt when we feel alone. Remember we are the most social species on the planet. It's baked into our DNA to hurt when we feel isolated from others. We all want to belong!

If you're skeptical, try this experiment: Ask a friend to cross their arms in pretend annoyance and then turn their back on you. Notice how just for a split second you felt a little touch of sadness or anger flare up in you even though you asked them to do it and you knew they were playing around. These feelings are real!

We would have all died in ancient times if we were cast out of the tribe.

Think about this scenario for a second:

You are living in prehistoric times. Something has gone wrong and you are cast out of your tribe. You are fending for yourself, trying to find food, shelter, and just generally trying to survive. You fall off of a cliff or outcropping and break your leg.

The plain truth is that you would most likely die. You would have needed the help of others to survive while you were healing and you would not be able to hunt for food or care for yourself.

These feelings of fear around being cast out at one time in our ancient past meant death. Now, this doesn't literally mean death, but it does result in more feelings of isolation which can feel pretty awful.

We all have strong emotions of sadness, fear, or anger that show up when we feel alone, rejected, and not part of the group. This is something that none of us gets any say about and that we all experience at times as human beings.

Remember, you are not alone.

Myth #3

You can tell what people are thinking and feeling just from looking at them.

You can't see people's thoughts and emotions from the outside. You can guess the emotions and thoughts of people around you, but often you will be wrong. Think about all of those times when you made a mistaken assumption about how someone was feeling.

We are all tempted to make assumptions from what we read on a text or even sometimes when we interact with people in person. Even when someone is right in front of you, we can still make mistakes. Someone may look sad—they are tearing up and we assume that something terrible has happened or they are very upset—when in reality their eyes are watering because the sun is really bright. Someone's face may look angry when in reality, they have an annoyed look because they have a headache. Or someone might be smiling wearing a mask of happiness when they are feeling like crying on the inside.

We all walk around at times feeling that we have this private inner struggle that no one else has. Being human is so tough because we have unlimited access to our own private mental experiences and no access to anyone else's! Other people are often playing it cool, pretending everything is all good.

We never truly have the opportunity to see or hear their inner thoughts and struggles, so how would we know that their inner thoughts look a lot like our inner thoughts?

The truth is, the struggles you are experiencing are actually what unifies you with all of humanity. So anytime you see another person in the world, you can know for certain that they too have difficult inner struggles and hard times even though you can't necessarily see them on the outside.

You are not alone.

Myth #4

We are so connected to everyone all the time with social media. This should make me feel connected, happy, and supported.

We are more physically isolated from each other today in the modern world than ever before, even though we are more connected to each other through our smartphones and the Internet.

Our phones and the Internet give us an illusion of being connected, but it doesn't really give us the true human face-to-face contact that we've evolved to truly need and crave. This is not to say that you should never use your phone or computer ever again. Our modern advances and technologies make many things easier for us in life, but we can't ignore the difficulties these technologies create either.

We are bringing this to your attention for one reason: through our well-intentioned attempts to feel connected through our phones and social media, we actually may be creating more isolation and a feeling of being down. This isn't our fault—it's what we have been taught. It's the technology we've been given. And it is a trap we all can become caught in so very easily.

You are not alone.

REFLECTION:

What thoughts and feelings show up when you think about these four myths?

What jumps out at you from your own life when you think about these myths?

We Are All in This Together: Our Common Humanity

So what do all of these myths mean when they are put together? We are really all in this together! Everyone struggles and everyone makes mistakes. We are all imperfect beings. We all stumble and we all fall down. To be truly human means that we are all a part of a common humanity.

But... sometimes it's hard for us to see this.

We feel alone, separated from everyone with our own personal struggles and imperfections. Sometimes we feel like no one could possibly understand what we are going through. The fact is, our struggles are not unique or separate even though it feels this way. The flaws we all have are part of being human and they are actually what connect us.

Carl Rogers, the renowned humanistic psychologist, had a powerful quote that is so true:

> "What is most personal is most general."

He understood that we are truly not alone with our perceived failures, flaws, challenges, and imperfections. The things that truly matter to us matter to others as well.

We as humans suffer more when we think that we are alone or if we think we are somehow not as lovable as other people.

On the other hand,

if we can remind ourselves that everyone falls and everyone makes mistakes, we can find comfort and strength to carry on when we are feeling down and alone.

Studies show that we actually self-correct faster with this approach rather than being hard on ourselves or even reminding ourselves that we are great.

Let's look at an example. Researchers at the University of Edinburgh in Scotland (Imogen Marsh, Stella Chan, and Angus Macbeth) published combined multiple research studies on self-compassion in young people in the journal *Mindfulness*. Their research focused on more than 7,000 adolescents from six countries, ranging in age from 10 to 19. They found that teens with high levels of self-compassion were most likely to have lower levels of distress caused by anxiety and depression—especially when facing persistent recurring academic pressure and stress (Marsh, Chan, MacBeth, 2018).

Even famous celebrities, musicians, and actors struggle—those people that look like they have perfect lives—and many are now having the courage to share this with the world. Famous people have the same evolved minds as we do and become caught in the same stuck places or loops that we do, despite what their social media feeds may look like. Here is just a short list of celebrities who have stepped up and embraced their humanity by sharing their struggles publicly.

We Are All in This Together: Actors, Musicians, Bands

Ryan Reynolds	Janet Jackson	Ariana Grande
Camila Cabello	Kendall Jenner	Adele
Prince Harry	Katy Perry	Lili Reinhart
Lena Dunham	Nicki Minaj	Kristen Stewart
Glenn Close	Camila Mendes	Kristen Bell
Zayn Malik	Sarah Silverman	Kerry Washington
Ellie Goulding	Olivia Munn	Amanda Seyfried
Cara Delevingne	J.K. Rowling	Selena Gomez
Halle Berry	Princess Diana	Gwyneth Paltrow
Beyoncé	Winona Ryder	Lady Gaga
Chrissy Teigen	Miley Cyrus	Michelle Williams
Dakota Johnson	Demi Lovato	Dwayne Johnson
Emma Stone	Carrie Fisher	Ellen DeGeneres
Jared Padalecki	Imagine Dragons	U2
X	We Banjo 3	Bruce Springsteen
Billie Eilish	Chance the Rapper	

This is a reminder that all human beings struggle and therefore compassion is needed! Compassion for others and compassion for ourselves.

We all get caught in mind traps with this tricky brain of ours—like comparing ourselves to others—and then we become stuck. These stuck places are like watching a fly that is caught in a glass bottle. It's not the fly's fault that it is stuck in the bottle. The fly is just doing what flies usually do—it's looking for food and in doing so flies into a bottle. The fly then attempts to do what usually works which is to fly straight ahead (remember, it's in a bottle which is clear so it looks like it could fly straight ahead and escape).

The poor fly ends up looping around and around until it accidentally does something that is not its first instinct, which is fly straight up and out of the bottle. So sometimes the way out of these stuck places is like showing the fly the way out of the bottle that none of us would really know unless someone told us. Even then it would take practice getting out of the bottle trap before it became more natural.

As we have discussed in chapters 1 and 2, the unexpected road out of these stuck places is mindful compassion. This tricky brain of ours with its old and new brain ways and its emotional systems often causes us to become caught up in these fly-in-the-bottle loops. We didn't choose the loops or what we've been given, but we live with it nonetheless.

We've already started down the road out of these stuck places. The beginning of the journey is understanding how our mind works and why we do the things we do.

In the next few chapters we will explore more about what we can do—the skills and mindful practices we can use on a daily basis—to free ourselves from these stuck places and begin to create positive changes in our lives.

The Important Stuff

✧ You are not alone.

✧ **Myth #1:** In order to have a good life you must be happy, confident, calm, and content all of the time. In reality, we live in a culture in which people pretend they are happy, confident, calm, and content all of the time. The fact that everyone is pretending to be happy all the time makes us feel that we are alone with our struggles, when actually we are not.

✧ **Myth #2:** You are weak if you feel sad when you are alone. In reality, we all hurt when we feel alone. Remember we are the most social species on the planet. It's baked into our DNA to hurt when we feel isolated from others.

✧ **Myth #3:** You can tell what people are thinking and feeling just from looking at them. In reality, you can't see people's thoughts and emotions from the outside. You can guess the emotions and thoughts of people around you, but often you will be wrong.

✧ **Myth #4:** We are so connected to everyone all the time with social media. This should make me feel connected, happy, and supported. In reality, we are more physically isolated from each other today in the modern world than ever before, even though we are more connected to each other through our smartphones and the Internet. Our phones and Internet give us an illusion of being connected, but it doesn't really give us the true human face-to-face contact that we've evolved to truly need and crave.

✧ Everyone struggles and everyone makes mistakes. We are all imperfect beings. We all stumble and we all fall down. To be truly human means that we are all a part of a common humanity. We all feel alone at times, separated from everyone with our own personal struggles and imperfections. Our struggles, though, are not unique or separate even though it feels this way. The flaws we all have are part of being human and they are actually what connect us.

For more resources, guided practices, and meditations, please visit our website: www.MindfulCompassionForTeens.com.

"When one tugs at a single thing in nature, she finds it attached to the rest of the world."

John Muir

Part Two

CHAPTER 4: Discovering What Is Important to Me
Practice #1: Following Your Bliss
Practice #2: The Wise Child

CHAPTER 5: Going for It!
Practice #3: Looking at Loops
Practice #4: Soothing Rhythm Breathing
Practice #5: Soothing Touch

CHAPTER 6: Help Is on the Way
Practice #6: Creating Your Compassionate Other
Practice #7: Taking Back the Wheel of the Ship with Your Compassionate Self
Practice #8: Letter from Your Compassionate Self
Practice #9: Gratitude Practice
Practice #10: Plan to Show Up as Your Highest Self
Practice #11: Escaping the Sleep Trap = Deep Rest

CHAPTER 7: Motivating with Kindness
Practice #12: Looking at Our Threat-Detecting Mind
Practice #13: Compassionate Playlist
Practice #14: Bringing Your Future Self to the Present
Practice #15: Loving Kindness Meditation
Practice #16: Where Are You in This Moment?
Practice #17: Becoming Your Compassionate Self
Practice #18: You Have Always Been Enough
Practice #19: Mindful Walking

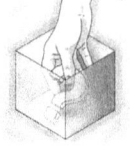

The Practices

CHAPTER 8: What Else Can I Do?

Practice #20: Your Best Self—Building Your Character
Practice #21: The Gift of Compassionate-Self Meditation
Practice #22: Mindful Doodle
Practice #23: Theme Song
Practice #24: Body Scan
Practice #25: Sitting Down in the Eye of the Storm
Practice #26: Dealing with Distractions

CHAPTER 9: Following the Spark

Practice #27: Soothing and Then Moving
Practice #28: Starting Again after Setbacks
Practice #29: Quick Restart
Practice #30: See Your Future Self
Practice #31: Stepping into Your Desired Future
Practice #32: Leaning into Fear with and without Support
Practice #33: Creating Slowing-Down Rituals

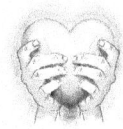

Discovering What Is Important to Me

"When a spider makes a beautiful web, the beauty comes out of the spider's nature. It's instinctive beauty. How much of the beauty of our own lives is about the beauty of being alive?"

Joseph Campbell

Curiosity Is a Beautiful Thing

It's not every day that someone asks,

"What's important to you?"

In fact, it's very rare that someone would ask you this question in a random daily conversation.

Whether we are aware of it or not, though, most of us try to live our lives based on what's important to us. For example, when we get up in the morning we probably don't say to ourselves, let's get out there and do meaningless stuff today! So because we are not asked this question very often you may be surprised that if you try to answer the question it may seem harder than you would think to answer. It's a question to be curious about though because it can really help us on our life path. **Let's give it a shot!**

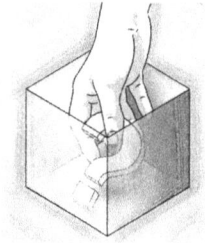

REFLECTION:

What's important to you?

Now a question that is also not very common for people to ask you directly is

"Who is important to you?"

(family, friends, coaches, teachers, pets, and even people who are no longer living)

Who is important to you in your life right now?

When we think about what and who is important
to us, what we are really doing is exploring our
values in a mindful way. Values are like a direction
to move towards rather than a set destination we
arrive at.

It's sort of like the early American pioneers heading west in their covered wagons. They would never actually arrive at the true west and if they tried to they would just end up circling the world.

If you find yourself not going in the direction you intended—maybe you start heading east instead of west—you can always stop and pull out your values as a compass and start heading west again.

Sometimes people confuse goals with values. Whereas values are a direction in life, goals are destinations—they are concrete and specific. An example of a goal would be running and finishing a 5k race for charity, whereas an example of a value is caring about physical wellness. As you can see, these are very different. Goals are a point on your life journey, and values are a direction that you can continually steer your life towards.

Your Inner Compass

Identifying what is important to you helps you to create your own inner compass. This compass then can help you with all of the decisions you have to make each day of our life. Your values are yours! People can take material things away from you—like your money, your car, your house, your phone—but they can't take your values away from you.

Another way of phrasing things that are important to you is bliss.

Remember that healthy Drive System that motivates you to action around the things that are important to you and the things that matter most? Bliss falls into that category. It's not just joy and happiness. Bliss is the stuff in life that has the deepest meaning and purpose for you. You feel drawn to these things naturally and you are willing to go through great trials and tribulations for them.

The prominent scholar Joseph Campbell, who influenced George Lucas's *Star Wars*, coined this important statement:

> "If you do follow your bliss you put yourself on a kind of track that has been there all the while, waiting for you... Follow your bliss ... and doors will open where you didn't know they were going to be. If you follow your bliss, doors will open for you that wouldn't have opened for anyone else."

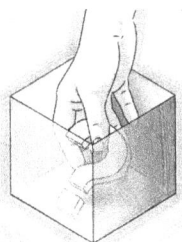

PRACTICE #1

Following Your Bliss

Let's create the points on your inner compass. What does "following your bliss" or your values mean to you at this moment in your life?

To help you identify your particular values by which you will steer your ship, here is a list of value words. Be curious and slow down—mindfully choose the words that speak to you. You will probably have a rather large list. After making your initial pass, take a look again and try to identify the 5-10 value words that are the MOST IMPORTANT to you at this point in your life. If you think of something that is not present on this list, feel free to add your own words in the space provided.

It's good to remember that your values may evolve and change over time—some things will remain the same, but others may shift as you live your life. So this list you are creating today is a snapshot of what is important to you right now.

Love (giving and receiving)
Spending time with people you care about
Being creative
Honesty
Pursuit of excellence
Appreciating beauty
Gratitude
Feeling joy
Learning
Wisdom
Physical movement or exercise

Self-acceptance
Forgiveness
Peace or calm
Integrity
Wonder
Compassion
Feeling safe
Having fun
Curiosity
Freedom
Self-expression

Protecting our environment
Living in the present moment
Following your dreams
Problem-solving

Savoring
Gentleness
Determination
Equality

Now that you have identified the values that are most important to you, think about how these show up in your daily life. Keep this list of your values handy. (You may want to take a picture of them with your phone so that you have them with you at all times.) In Chapter 5: Going for It, we will talk more about how we can move towards our valued path, living our values daily, with intention, mindfulness, and self-compassion.

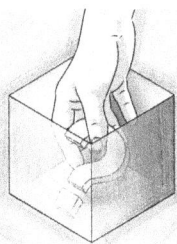

PRACTICE #2

The Wise Child

Another way to help you discover what is important to you is to take a moment to reflect back to when you were a young child.

Close your eyes and activate your Soothing System by beginning to breathe slowly and intentionally in a rhythm that feels good to your body. We call this soothing rhythm breathing and will ask you to breathe in this way in many of the practices throughout this book. To start this soothing rhythm breathing, breathe in slowly through your nose for a count of four and out slowly through your mouth (as if you were blowing through a very large straw) for a count of four. As you slowly breathe, add in a warm half-smile (the kind of smile you have when you see a good friend or family member you haven't seen for a while). This lets your body and mind know that all is well.

> Keep breathing like this for a few moments until you begin to feel the sensation of slowing down.

Now imagine yourself as a young child and see yourself in your mind's eye. Remember times when you felt the most joy and peace. Think about the things you loved playing as a child. Remember whether you enjoyed playing more inside or outside. See these images in your mind and remember all the details of what you were doing and who was with you. Where were you? Take your time and linger over all the details you can recall. Now mentally record all of these details and bring them all back with you.

What did you see in your time of imagining?
Draw a picture or write down what you saw.

Remembering What's Important to You

What showed up in this practice of The Wise Child are clues which you can use to discover or rediscover what is important to you. Remember, we all come into this world with gifts, joys, and abilities, but sometimes they become covered up or forgotten over time.

One of the most famous psychologists in history, Carl Jung, discovered this after he had a difficult time in his life. Carl was working with the father of modern psychology, Sigmund Freud. Carl and Sigmund had different opinions that eventually led to the end of their professional relationship. Carl was very upset and wasn't sure about what to do with the next chapter of his life so he thought back to what he loved most as a young child.

He remembered that he loved making sand castles as a boy. Carl bought a run-down old cottage and decided to hire Italian stonemasons to help him fix it up. Carl worked alongside the stonemasons as he built his own little castle of sorts on a lake in Switzerland. Over many years Carl would work on his little cottage with his own hands. Carl said when he was working on his cottage he felt most himself and at peace.

We can take a hint from Carl and go back to rediscover what truly brings us joy and a sense of well-being. Obviously, we all can't hire Italian stonemasons to help us build our own chalet in Switzerland, but we all do have the ability to reconnect with something from our past that gave us great joy and bring it into our lives now.

When we discover these things, we can begin on our own authentic path of building what would bring us joy, contentment, and fulfillment.

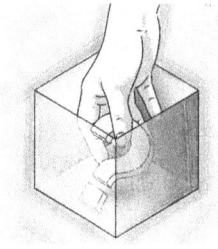

REFLECTION:

Now that you have these images from your past, let's bring them into the future of today. Write down the images that came up from your childhood and then brainstorm ways you can do something similar in your life now.

Images from Your Childhood Today	Brainstorm for Your Life
1.	1.
2.	2.
3.	3.

You can rekindle and reawaken these things you have loved again and again. You can reinvent them and bring them into your life now and in the future in whatever way feels best.

The Important Stuff

✧ Become curious about who and what is important to you right now in your life.

✧ When we think about who and what is important to us, what we are really doing is exploring our values. Values are like a direction to move towards rather than a set destination where we arrive at some point in our lives.

✧ Sometimes people confuse goals with values. Whereas values are a direction in life, goals are destinations—they are concrete and specific.

✧ Identifying what is important to you helps you to create your own inner compass. This compass then can help you with all of the decisions you have to make each day of your life. Your values are yours! People can take material things away from you—like your money, your car, your house, your phone—but they can't take your values away from you.

For more resources, guided practices, and meditations, please visit our website:
www.MindfulCompassionForTeens.com.

-69-

"You cannot get through a single day without having an impact on the world around you. What you do makes a difference, and you have to decide what kind of difference you want to make."

Dr. Jane Goodall

Going for It!

"You can't stop the waves, but
you can learn to surf."

Dr. Jon Kabat-Zinn

Moving Towards or Away

We have evolved to get away from things that can hurt us. So when we
come into contact with stuff that is uncomfortable (like when we are trying
new things that we value or trying something that is challenging, but also
that is something we love) we all want to get away from the uncomfortable
thoughts and emotions that these experiences create.

We are all still here on this planet because we had ancestors who knew
when to hide, fight, or run away. Those folks who didn't know how to keep
themselves safe don't have descendants! So each day—whether we know it
or not—we try to move towards what's important to us, but often we run
into difficult situations where we are triggered to run away, hide, or freeze.

So what do we do at those times when we have this primitive impulse
to run away or hide or freeze? At these points we have a choice to move
towards what we value or move away from what we value. Most of the
time, though, we don't realize we even have a choice.

The Wisdom of Our Compassionate Self

Remember from our values discussion in Chapter 4 (Discovering What's Important to Me), a compass helps us find our way when we are unsure of which way to go and points us in the right direction (north, south, east, and west).

> The wisdom of our Compassionate Self points us in the direction of our values and then provides us with the insight on how to mindfully move towards these values, regardless of what is going on in our heads (inner world) or in the world around us (outer world).

Let's describe for a moment what we mean by our inner world. When someone looks at you they are not able to see what's going on inside—your thoughts, feelings, or bodily sensations—and you can't see what's going on inside of them either. We each have an inner world of rapidly changing thoughts, emotions, and bodily experiences that only we have access to. It is also important to note that no one can see what is important to you by looking at you from the outside.

No one can see inside our heads!

When we take action steps towards the things that are most important to us (our values), our inner world of emotions and thoughts often shows up strongly. When this happens we often stop in our tracks and try to avoid the difficult emotions and thoughts. Our old brain gets tricked into perceiving these thoughts as facts or real dangers.

As we spoke about earlier, this is because our old brain is so easily deceived by the new brain's ability to think, imagine, and project into the future or past. The old emotional brain interprets these inner thoughts as fact and then believes these inner thoughts are dangerous and things to avoid. The problem—as you can see—is that we can become trapped or stuck by these difficult thoughts and the back-and-forth loops in our heads. This trap can keep us from living the life we love and from doing the things we dream to do!

Thoughts Are Just Thoughts

It takes courage to go for what's truly important to you in life. Your mind may tell you quite often that you don't have courage, but that is not the truth. It's just a thought. And what we are doing here in this book is creating a new way of being, a way to be free from what your mind has been telling you.

Let's imagine we are walking in the woods on a beautiful day. We are having such a great conversation that we don't notice a large stick on the path and as we walk over it we trip and fall to the ground. You quickly stand up because you are not actually hurt, just surprised and startled, but I lay on the ground and start beating myself in the head with the stick that we just stumbled over. Shocked, you ask me what am I doing. I tell you that I'm learning and that I have to beat myself with this stick in order to learn to pay more attention while I'm walking in the woods. You say that's nuts and tell me to stop. I say,

> "Well how am I going to learn then?"

This story sounds a bit absurd when we are reading it, but this is what we actually do when we make mistakes in life. We fall down (make a mistake) and we instinctively beat ourselves up in order to motivate ourselves.

So why do we do this? Think back to the old-brain and new-brain loop. When we turn on ourselves like this, the old-brain Threat System is just doing its job (trying to keep us safe), but it hurts us in the process.

We see something in ourselves we don't like and we attack it just as we would attack a predator that has backed us into a corner. Again, when you look at this scenario in the context of our old brains, it's easy to see why it's not our fault that we criticize ourselves in this way!

The tricky catch in all of this is that when we attack ourselves with self-critical thoughts, we activate our Threat System. And it is much harder to self-correct and think calmly and rationally when our Threat System is activated and we feel scared, anxious, stressed, or angry—remember all of our attention is hyper-focused on that threat.

Imagine trying to do math while being chased or eaten by a grizzly bear—not going to happen, right? The old brain is so easily tricked into believing that self-critical thoughts are actually real concrete threats. However, by knowing this we can create a different option for ourselves.

> We can do something that can actually help us return toward our value-driven path of what's important to us.

The Loops in Our Heads

As we are attempting to live a good life—or when we are just trying to survive—we will all experience these loops in our heads. This may sound funny but we all get caught up in the back and forth. We've talked about this a bit, but let's dive in a little deeper.

> The loop goes like this: We first have a self-critical thought in our new brain that then loops down to the old brain. This kicks in our primitive emotion that then fires up the new brain with another inner critical thought or image, and it goes round and round, on and on.

As you can see, the old-brain emotions are very powerful but not wise (Kolts, 2016). The old-brain emotions strongly influence what we focus on, think about, and imagine. Remember our dog Coco, little Chucky, and McLovin? While that was an example of external situations impacting the brain, now think about how this might happen both from real things happening around us and from an inner self-critical standpoint as well.

For example, you're looking in the mirror doing your hair and your new brain has the thought: My hair looks like crap! That thought then loops down to the old brain and triggers fear and anger because your mind can quickly jump from that subjective (not fact) self-critical opinion of

"My hair looks like crap" to "If I go to school with my hair like this people are going to make fun of me or worse."

This thought then loops back up to your new brain and creates more images of being laughed at or rejected by friends. See how easy it is to go from one self-critical thought to being caught in an upsetting round-and-round in your brain?

We all have these loops because we all have this tricky brain between our ears. We can begin to name our loops and begin to free ourselves from them over time with practice and mindful awareness.

The thing is, this happens with lots of everyday thoughts, but as we do things that are more challenging and engage in activities that really matter to us, these loops happen more often. When we are going for our dreams or even just setting the stage to go for it, our tricky brain kicks in big time. Why? Our brain wants to keep us safe—wants to ensure our survival, and when we do new things outside of our comfort zone our tricky brain is triggered to keep things safely the same.

Breaking Free of the Loops

One alternative to help us break free from the loops in our mind is to name the difficult emotion, soothe it, and then move towards what is important to us in our purpose-driven life.

As you soothe your body and mind you will begin to shift into your safeness system. With a little practice, this safeness will comfort you, your thoughts will become less threat-based, and it will then be easier to move forward in all areas of your life.

The unwanted difficult thoughts that may still remain can be compared to dogs that bark at you, but never bite. You learn in time to walk past the dogs while they bark at you rather than turning around and heading home or just stopping. One way you can handle these barking-dog thoughts is to name what the barking thoughts are in a creative way. For example saying to yourself,

"My mind is telling me that I'm not good enough."

Saying this to yourself when challenging thoughts come up is a new alternative to reacting to those barking dogs and believing that this thought is a fact.

Let's look at these thoughts for a moment. Just because you have the thought, "I'm a lamp" does not mean that the room you are sitting in will be any brighter. By mindfully coming back to the present moment and noticing that a thought is showing up (**by saying "my mind is telling me that…"**) gives you space and freedom to keep walking even with these yapping dog thoughts!

> Remember we have this old brain that is easily tricked into believing that thoughts are real threats. This means that all of us at times will become hooked into believing that thoughts are threats, but they aren't threats, they are just thoughts.

This feeling of safeness and not reacting to thoughts gives us courage. Our Australian psychologist friend Dr. James Kirby says it is like mountain climbing, we first have to create the feeling of safeness before we begin to climb. You strap into your harness and then make sure it is secure. This experience of knowing you're safely supported by your harness allows you to start climbing.

The Compassionate Self's wisdom shows us again that it is not our fault that we get stuck in these traps (Gilbert & Choden, 2014). The cool thing is that with this wisdom and these tools you can choose to climb whatever mountain in life you wish! The Compassionate Self's wisdom shows us that we can keep climbing that mountain towards our values regardless of what difficult thoughts and emotions show up along the way.

"Keep climbing that mountain, keep looking up, and in the stillness of your thoughts you will find comfort and the will to carry on."

Bobby Fraser

Name to Tame

There is a saying coined by Dr. Daniel J. Siegel, "Name it, to tame it." What he is saying here is that naming the difficult emotion fear, sadness, anger, disgust is the first step to releasing yourself from that old-brain, new-brain loop. **We would like to change that saying to name it, soothe it, move it. So if you can name it you can soothe it, and then if you can soothe it you can learn to move it towards what is important in life.**

It is not our fault that we get caught in loops. It's just what happens as we live our lives with this tricky brain. Everyone (we really do mean EVERYONE) has this challenge of getting caught in loops. And by soothing and slowing down we allow ourselves to better deal with and tolerate the distress we are experiencing.

> We are not suggesting that we need to avoid or banish these difficult thoughts, feelings, and emotions, but we can learn by soothing to better tolerate and balance what comes up.

By identifying how this tricky brain of ours works, in time you can begin to take this awareness of your loops out into your daily life. This knowledge and understanding will give you the power to mindfully navigate the storms that inevitably come up in day-to-day life much more effectively than ever before.

The image that comes to mind when we think about these loops in our brains is the old-fashioned car "ride" at an amusement park. If you've ever been on one of these "rides" it seems cool to be driving an old car until you realize you can't really go anywhere except on this path with the guide rail. When you try to drive in a different direction you are continually bounced back by the rail to stay on the little path when what you'd really like to do is drive around the whole park! Driving around in circles on one little path isn't that much fun when you can see all of the places you could go, but don't have access to.

Breaking free of these loops is like learning to jump the old-fashioned car off the track so you can go anywhere you want in the park of life. How very cool would that be! It's one thing to think about doing this for a ride, but it's even cooler to know that we can learn to do this and go anywhere we want to in life.

PRACTICE #3:

Looking at Loops

Dr. Chris Irons from London, England, has a practice that helps us break free from the loops we all experience. First, take a look at the example below of a common loop that we all may get caught up in at times. Then, reflect on some of the thinking and feeling loops that you get caught up in. Allow yourself to be curious. Identify the loops that are particularly difficult for you right now.

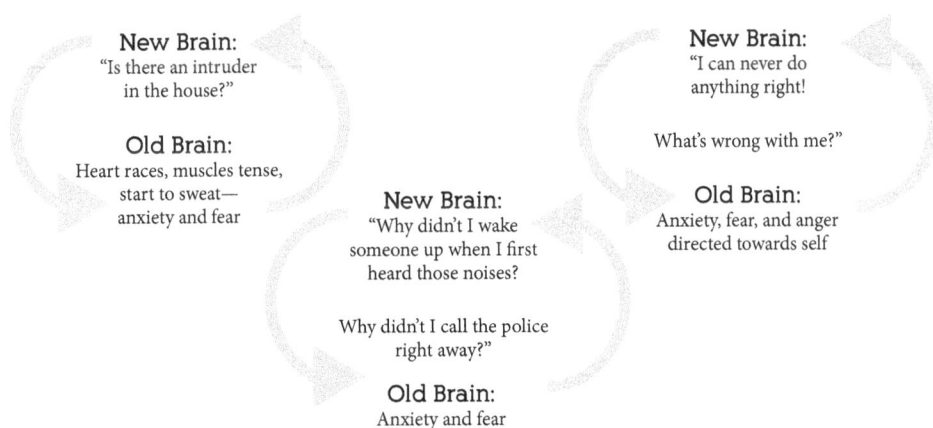

New Brain:
"Is there an intruder in the house?"

Old Brain:
Heart races, muscles tense, start to sweat—
anxiety and fear

New Brain:
"Why didn't I wake someone up when I first heard those noises?

Why didn't I call the police right away?"

Old Brain:
Anxiety and fear

New Brain:
"I can never do anything right!

What's wrong with me?"

Old Brain:
Anxiety, fear, and anger directed towards self

What are some of the old brain, new brain loops that you see in your life and are particularly difficult right now for you?

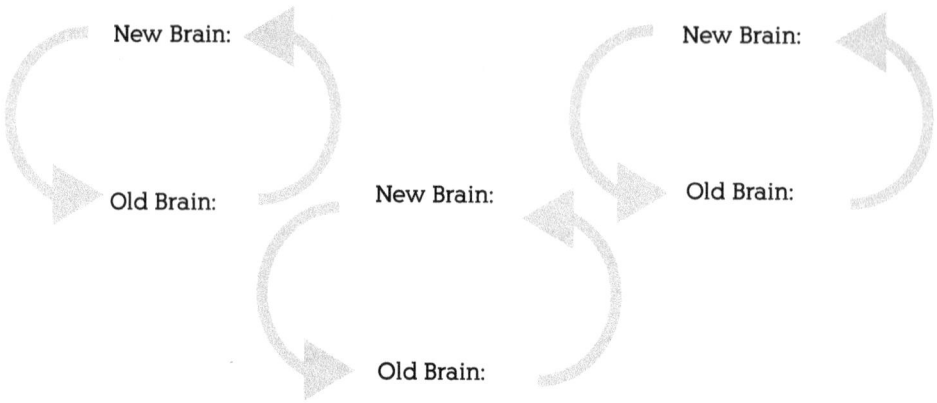

New Brain:

New Brain:

Old Brain:

New Brain:

Old Brain:

Old Brain:

Now that you have named and identified some of the difficult thoughts that challenge you, we can begin to practice mindfully slowing down and soothing ourselves, and then you'll be able to really go for what's truly important in your life.

As you are going about your day, you may even want to mentally whisper the word "loop" when one shows up and begins to spiral in your mind. Allow yourself to notice, pay attention, and be mindful as these thoughts and feelings show up. You could even pretend that you are secretly taking a hook out of your mouth like a fish that has been caught. In doing this, you will be reminding yourself not to get hooked by the new brain's attempt to bait the old brain into reacting. Be creative and come up with your own ways of breaking out of these old-brain and new-brain loops. Try different things and see what feels best to you!

"Between stimulus and response, there is a space. In that space is our power to choose our response. In our response lies our growth and our freedom."

Victor Frankl, M.D., holocaust survivor

Soothe

"Breathing in, I calm body and mind. Breathing out, I smile. Dwelling in the present moment I know this is the only moment."

THÍCH NHAT HANH

The first thing (and simplest) we can do to soothe and balance our minds is slow rhythm breathing. Slowing our breathing down sends a message to our brain that we are not in true danger at this very moment and gives us a sense of inner safeness. This inner safeness then allows us to look at our surroundings and gives us the courage to explore the things we might fear or worry about.

Out of this sense of safeness we have created, we can then begin to take committed action steps towards those things in life that are most important to us.

PRACTICE #4:

Soothing Rhythm Breathing

Steps:

1. Breathe in through your nose slowly for a count of three to five seconds and smoothly out through your nose or mouth for the count of three to five seconds.

2. Now bring a warm and friendly smile to your face as if you are seeing a good friend or pet you haven't seen for a long time.

3. On the exhale say to yourself with a gentle and supportive inner voice the words: slowing down, slowing down, slowing down.

4. Focus on breathing right down into your diaphragm, allowing your belly to relax and expand like a balloon and then letting it deflate like a balloon when you breathe out.

5. After breathing this way for one or two minutes, bring your attention to the effect this slow rhythm breathing has had on your body and your mind.

To start with you may want to begin with just 30 seconds of this slow-down breathing three times a day.

Some people may feel a little wound up or agitated when they first try to slow their breathing down. Please remember that there is nothing wrong with you if this is your experience. The Threat System is just saying,

"Hey don't slow down your breathing because that will put your guard down and then we might not be safe."

Many of us are so used to the fast pace go, go, go of modern life that it takes practice and time to eventually comfort our nervous system. But with gentle, persistent practice the body and mind will know that it is actually safe to to go into the soothe, rest, and digest mode rather than the threat and drive mode it is so used to.

What did you notice in your body and your mind as you were practicing this slow rhythm breathing? How do you feel now after completing this practice?

PRACTICE #5:

Soothing Touch

As humans, we have the longest infancy of any mammal. Human beings can't fend for themselves for a very long time as compared to other animals. We need to be held, swaddled, rocked, and comforted as babies. None of us popped out of the womb and started running around asking for a burrito. In contrast, think about a baby horse that is up and running around a few minutes after it is born.

We have evolved to all need soothing touch and loving gentle voices. Soothing touch calms and comforts children and reminds them that they are safe. And the need for soothing touch doesn't stop after infancy for us. We need soothing touch from the moment we are born until the moment we take our last breath (Gilbert & Choden, 2014).

Like soothing rhythm breathing, soothing touch works to calm and comfort our nervous system (Neff, 2011). Think about a young child just learning to walk who falls down hard and begins to cry. How would you comfort them? Maybe with a gentle touch on the cheek or by picking them up with a warm hug. The child would be calmed and soothed by your caring touch.

It is also important to point out that after we are soothed we can discover a renewed strength that helps us move forward.

Now let's see which kind of soothing touch is most comforting, soothing, and strengthening for you!

Try each of these out. After each one take a moment to pause and notice how it feels to you. There is no right or wrong here, only what feels best in the moment. You can even combine some of these ideas or come up with your own if these suggestions fall short for you.

✧ Place an opened hand over your heart. Feel the weight and warmth of your hand on your chest.

✧ Place both hands over your heart. Try placing one hand over the top of the other.

✧ Place a gentle hand on the side of your cheek or try gently stroking your cheek.

✧ Cross your arms and give yourself a warm hug and hold it for a moment.

✧ Make a fist and put it over your heart and then place the other hand over top.

✧ Gently pat yourself on the heart.

✧ Pet your hair as if you are a child being soothed at bed time.

✧ Place both hands on each side of your face and allow your face to be gently held.

✧ Hold one of your hands in a supportive way.

✧ Give yourself a pat on the back or a gentle pat on the back of the head.

✧ Place a hand under your underarm and the other hand over the opposite arm and give yourself a little hug.

✧ Place your hands on your stomach with one hand over another.

Which soothing touch was most soothing to you?
Which ones felt the best?

Describe how you felt when you used this soothing
touch?

Throughout your day notice when you are feeling upset and practice
combining soothing rhythm breathing with the soothing touch that feels
best for you.

It's good to keep in mind that the soothing touch that feels good to you now may change over time, so please give yourself permission to change it up once in awhile to see what feels best in the moment.

The Important Stuff

✧ It takes courage to go for what's truly important to you in life. Your mind may tell you quite often that you don't have courage, but that is not the truth. It's just a thought. You don't have to believe what your mind has been telling you. We can create a different option for ourselves. We can do something that can actually help us return toward our purpose-driven path of what's important to us.

✧ We all experience loops in these tricky brains of ours. Sometimes the loops cause us to attack ourselves with self-critical thoughts and images.

✧ We have evolved to protect ourselves from things that can hurt us. When we come into contact with difficult experiences (even if they are things we value or love) we all want to get away from the uncomfortable thoughts and emotions that come up. At these points we have a choice to move towards what we value or move away from what we value.

✧ We can deal with uncomfortable thoughts and emotions by naming the difficult emotion, soothing it, and then moving towards what is important to us.

✧ As you soothe your body and mind you will begin to shift into your safeness system. We are not suggesting that you need to soothe your problems away. We soothe so that we may better tolerate the distress we experience. With a little practice, this safeness will comfort you, your thoughts will become less threat-based, and it will then be easier to move forward in all areas of your life.

✧ The easiest and simplest way to soothe and balance our minds is to mindfully slow our breathing. Slowing our breathing down sends a message to our brain that we are not in true danger at this very moment and gives us a sense of inner safeness. This inner safeness then allows us to explore our surroundings and gives us the courage to explore the things we might fear or worry about. Out of this sense of safeness we have created, we can then begin to take committed action steps towards those things in life that are most important to us.

For more resources, guided practices, and meditations, please visit our website:
www.MindfulCompassionForTeens.com.

Going for It!   -92-

"Start where you are. Use what
you have. Do what you can."

Arthur Ashe

Help Is on the Way

chapter 6

"We were scared, but our
fear was not as strong as our
courage."

Malala Yousafzai

Using Imagery

As you probably have seen from our discussions about our old-brain and
new-brain loops, imagery plays a very important role in our lives and how
we feel on a moment-to-moment basis even if we don't realize it. We are
constantly creating images in our heads from the past and from what might
happen in the future. While the images in our heads sometimes have the
power to stop us in our tracks, we can also use our ability to create imagery
to help move us towards what is most important to us in our lives.

Imagery can bring our Soothing
System online or it also can
be used to activate our Drive
System when we really need to
take action on something we care
about.

So what is imagery and how can we use it to our advantage?

As you may remember from our talk about the old brain and the new brain, the old brain is not very good at telling the difference between things that are happening in the outside world (in real life) and the thoughts, images, and fantasies in our mind. The good news is we can use this ability to create and see images in our mind to help us. Purposely using imagery—on our own terms—is a powerful way to influence our mood and develop compassionate strength.

And remember, compassion is more than kindness. According to Dr. Paul Gilbert,

> compassion is "the sensitivity to pain and suffering in yourself or others and a commitment and motivation to try to alleviate that suffering or prevent it."

We imagine things all the time in our day-to-day life without even realizing it. Think about it. We have all made a mistake or had an argument with someone and then minutes, hours, or even days later the images of that mistake or conflict play over and over again in our minds. These images seem to come at us fast and hard and we feel like we have no control over them, but what if we could practice some equally powerful imagery that helped us to feel safe and loved?

Start small. At first, this can be difficult because we automatically try to create sharp and distinct pictures in our mind's eye. But it's not really important to see everything in such a clear way. It doesn't have to look like a movie or video game. What IS important is to create mental experiences that can help you activate compassion and a sense of safeness in your mind. For example, you may imagine someone you love dearly and you may not have a clear mental picture of them, but rather an experience of warmth and a feeling of being supported nonetheless.

One powerful way we can use imagery to soothe ourselves is to create a picture of what we call our Compassionate Other and our Compassionate Self.

The Compassionate Other: What Is It?

I've Got Your Back

The Compassionate Other is like a superhero's loyal sidekick that always has their back! We are going to use our new brain's capacity for imagination to bring our Compassionate Other out in full force. But first, we have to create it and understand why we are creating it.

Research by Dr. James A. Coan has shown that when we have a trusted friend with us, we perceive challenges as less overwhelming. He even found that physical pain is reduced in our bodies when a close friend holds our hand when we are experiencing it. So we have found that even imagining that someone's got our back calms us and gives us both strength and courage. Doing a little of your own research, you can reflect back on your life and remember a time when a friend has told you, "I've got your back" (or when you had a deep sense that they did even if they didn't say it out loud) or when they said, "I'm here for you" and how great it felt.

PRACTICE #6:

Creating Our Compassionate Other

Compassion Focused Therapy has created the idea of developing our Compassionate Other. If you are willing, please close your eyes and begin your soothing rhythm breathing. Slowing your breathing down slows down the body and the mind.

Bring to your mind an image of a person, animal, or being that would accept you just as you are. Remember we are just imagining. If you are having the thought that a person like that doesn't exist, you can allow yourself to let go of that thought.

Think about your Compassionate Other in detail. What does the image of your Compassionate Other look like? Is it human or animal? Is it young or old? What are they wearing? What colors are associated with this image?

Notice the qualities of this Compassionate Other. (understanding, nonjudgmental, warm, wise, kind, mature, loving, steadfast, loyal, playful, attentive, caring)

Now imagine that you meet your Compassionate Other in a place that represents safeness, calmness, and beauty to you. Notice the sounds, the colors, the smells, and the feel of this place where you meet your Compassionate Other.

Imagine as you walk towards your Compassionate Other you feel a sense of warmth.

Imagine your Compassionate Other hugs you and that you can feel their love all around you.

Let the warmth, love, and sense of protection soak
into every cell of your body.

By visualizing and imagining our Compassionate Other, we are tapping
into our mind's ability to activate compassion that soothes us. As we are
soothed, we can find the strength to do what's important to us. Being
soothed by our Compassionate Other imagery greatly helps us to tolerate
the distress we will naturally experience when we are moving towards what
is important to us.

Describe or draw (or both) what you imagine for
your Compassionate Other. What did you notice
about this being? When you met your Compassionate
Other in that place of safeness, calmness, and beauty,
what did you see, feel, and notice?

The Compassionate Self: What Is It?

If the Compassionate Other is the superhero sidekick, the Compassionate Self is like the superhero self we wear under our everyday clothes. It's the best version of ourselves. Those superheroes often look like ordinary people from the outside, but they have amazing powers on the inside.

Compassion Focused Therapy again talks about developing and also nurturing our Compassionate Self.

The four core qualities of our Compassionate Self are the same as most superheroes. These core qualities are wisdom, caring-commitment, strength, and courage!

Getting in touch with your Compassionate Self is a lot like an actor getting into a role for a movie. The actor first brings to mind the qualities of the character they are playing and then they practice acting like the character. They walk, talk, and even try to think like the character they are playing.

There have been studies with actors being placed into brain scans as they act out certain emotions and we can see their brains change as they act out these emotions. Therefore, we can create real brain changes—and changes in our lives—if we practice becoming our most compassionate version of ourselves over time. We can practice trying on the Compassionate Self outfit as something we can do to embody this most compassionate version of ourselves.

Imagining ourselves at our compassionate best helps us become more like this version of ourselves. As we bring these images to our mind and practice walking around like this during our day, we can imagine how this compassionate version of ourselves interacts with others. We can see the detail of how they move, their facial expressions, the clothes they wear, their posture, voice, and even the look in their eyes. We also can imagine that this version of ourselves has unconditional love and concern for us no matter what.

The Compassionate Self has your back 100%!

It can tolerate great distress on your behalf and provides unlimited support for you. We don't even realize it but we unconsciously put on different versions of ourselves all the time. For example, we put on a different version of ourselves for our grandparents than we do for our friends. We can learn to put on our Compassionate Self with a little practice anytime and anywhere.

The Wisdom of the Compassionate Self

The Compassionate Self is the watcher or the observer self that has deep wisdom. The Compassionate Self has the ability to:

- ✧ View thoughts as thoughts (not facts).
- ✧ Unhook from sticky or difficult and persistent thoughts.
- ✧ Notice when you are moving towards or away from your values.
- ✧ Notice unhelpful avoidant ways that you deal with unwanted inner thoughts and feelings.
- ✧ Support you unconditionally.

The wise Compassionate Self understands how our Threat System influences the thoughts and feelings we experience. The Compassionate Self helps us to remember to soothe and then encourages us to move in our valued direction of our purpose-driven life.

As we choose to move towards what is most important in our lives, we will all have many difficult emotions or parts of ourselves try to distract us from our values. Really they are just getting in our way. These parts of ourselves will attempt to influence us to go in a different direction away from what we value.

Our friend Dr. Russell Kolts at Eastern Washington University says we can think of our mind as a ship at sea. On this ship we all have "crew members" who represent different emotions that try to take control of the ship at times. For example, our anxious self may grab the the wheel of the ship and turn away from asking that special person out on a date. Your sad inner critic may put you down and keep you from breaking up with a person who treats you poorly.

The good news is that with a little practice we can learn to train the compassionate part of our minds to be the captain of the ship. The Compassionate Self can calm down the difficult parts of ourselves that try to take over our lives.

PRACTICE #7:

Taking Back the Wheel of the Ship with Your Compassionate Self

Step 1: Notice who has taken over the ship. (Oh, it's you angry self.)

Step 2: Slow down your breathing. Breathe in slowly for five seconds and then exhale slowly for five seconds. At the same time, gently tell yourself in your mind, "slowing down, slowing down, slowing down." Take your time with slowing down here. Don't rush it. The more you slow down, the easier it will be to summon the image of your Compassionate Self.

Step 3: Imagine becoming your Compassionate Self. Imagine all the traits of your Compassionate Self (wise, kind, patient, strong) just like you're watching a movie. Imagine growing stronger and feeling supported from the inside.

Step 4: Embody (become) your Compassionate Self. Pretend you are your Compassionate Self in this moment. A wise and seasoned sea captain knows that emotional storms are just part of sailing the seas of life and knows how to navigate them. So now imagine yourself saying (as the Compassionate Self to your angry self),

"You can be here angry self,
but you are not taking over
this ship because we are going
somewhere that is important to
us."

Step 5: Let the other parts of ourselves just come along for the ride. The Compassionate Self can calm the other parts of ourselves that try to create mutiny at times. The Compassionate Self doesn't have to make angry self or anxious self go away. The Compassionate Self has enough soothing and tolerance for everyone and can hold everyone in a place of safeness.

With practice we can learn to put the Compassionate Self at the wheel of the ship of life and just let the other parts go along for the ride. The Compassionate Self then can choose to take their advice if it helps us go to where we truly want to go in life (Gilbert & Choden, 2014).

Be patient yet persistent with this practice. At first you may think this whole thing with the Compassionate Self is silly or stupid. Just give it some time and you will notice gradual positive changes.

PRACTICE #8:

Letter from your Compassionate Self

Now that you have seen how you can make your Compassionate Self the captain of your ship, imagine your Compassionate Self writing you a letter of support. A letter from your Compassionate Self is a very effective and helpful way to give yourself support and bring you to a place of safeness and calm (Kolts, 2016).

First, start to hear this letter in your mind, the kind and supportive words that you would receive. What positive things would this calm and Compassionate Self say to you? Notice not only the words, but also the supportive tone of the letter.

Write this letter to yourself. Don't worry about spelling or punctuation. Just let it pour out onto the page.

Starting Your Day on the Good Foot

Starting your day off on the good foot means that we can make a move towards our values and purpose before we even get out of bed. When we open our eyes in the morning the mind often starts immediately into the to-do lists and the cares of the day.

What if you made the choice to do something different? What if you learned to practice tuning before you play the concert of your life?

Even the best musicians need to tune before they play. One of the ways we tune is to begin to break out of our minds' evolved program to search for the negatives. How do we break out of that program? Start the day with a gratitude practice.

PRACTICE #9:

Gratitude Practice

As soon as you open your eyes, allow yourself to be mindfully present in this moment. Think about five things for which you are grateful. Use your fingers on one hand to count these five things. If five feels impossible to you, start with two or three. And if that feels like you just can't do it, start with one. Eventually you can work your way up to ten things for which you are grateful.

It may sound simple, but it is powerful.

These ten things don't need to be huge, life-changing, save-the-world things, but a mix of big and little things.

For example, I'm thankful for my friends, hot showers, my family, spell-check, nice-smelling soap, coffee, and so on. While you are listing these things you're grateful for, also reflect on why you are grateful. Sometimes even things that we think would be difficult to be grateful for end up being huge teachers and game changers for us. This is important to pay attention to and think about. And if you love to journal you can also write your gratitudes down in a notebook that you keep next to your bed. It's up to you and you can't do it wrong!

Let's try it now. List, draw, or doodle some of the things for which you are grateful right now in this moment.

PRACTICE #10:

Plan to Show Up as Your Highest Self

The next way to start the day off on the good foot is to take a moment after your gratitudes and create a movie in your mind of how you would like to show up today. Imagine how you would like to live today as the best version of yourself—maybe your Compassionate Self.

Our dear friend Dr. Dennis Tirch gave Chris this assignment to do each morning. Chris noticed over time that starting his days off this way began to help him be his best self more of the time throughout his days.

The practice starts with imagining that you are watching yourself on video embodying this best version of you. Notice the values and traits that this highest version of you is living out (friendly, kind, funny). Watch how this highest version of you interacts with others. Listen to what this version of you says or chooses not to say. Even take notice of the tone of voice and your body posture (how you are sitting, standing, walking, or moving). Next, imagine that you are becoming this highest version of yourself as you lay there under the covers.

So when you actually get out of bed and feel your feet touch the floor you are now imagining you actually are this highest version of yourself. Take on this Compassionate Self body posture—the way you hold your body when you are standing, sitting, walking, or moving in this highest version of yourself—like an actor preparing for a role in a play or a movie. This may mean that you are standing straighter or taller with your shoulders back, feeling strong and confident in your body or it may mean something different for you. Experiment with what your Compassionate Self body posture means to you.

How do you feel when you imagine yourself as this highest version of yourself? Do you notice any differences in your physical body as you practice this?

Remember, anytime throughout your day when you become aware that you are drifting away from living this version of yourself, you can nonjudgmentally return to embodying or becoming this highest version of yourself. How do we do that? By slowing down our breathing, mindfully coming back to the present moment, and then acting as if we are this highest self.

You can purposely take on the Compassionate Self body posture, voice tone, and behavior of this highest self at any time during your day.

Shakespeare said life is a play, so let the play of your life begin!

Impermanence = This Too Shall Pass

Everything in life is constantly changing.

When we are heading towards our dreams and values it is helpful to remember this. If we just think about the weather for a moment, or look at pictures of ourselves from the past, we can actually see that everything is constantly changing. The challenging moments, emotions, and thoughts all will pass as you move compassionately in your valued life direction. Just having this knowledge and giving ourselves this gentle reminder on our path of life can be so helpful.

There is a very famous and ancient story about this truth. According to this story, there once lived a powerful king. The king was continuously torn between happiness and depression. The smallest things could make him really upset or give him an intense emotional reaction, so his happiness easily turned into disappointment and despair. One day the king became tired of himself and started seeking a way out.

He sent for a woman known for being one of the wisest people in his kingdom. When she arrived, the king said to her,

"I want to be like you. Can you bring me something that gives balance, peace, and serenity in my life? I will pay whatever price you like."

The wisewoman replied,

"I may be able to help you, but the price is so great that not even your kingdom would be enough payment for it. Therefore I will give it to you as a gift, if you will honor it."

The king gave his promise, and the wisewoman left. A few weeks later she returned, and handed the king an ornate box carved in jade. The king opened the box, and found a simple gold ring inside. The inscription on the ring read, This, too, shall pass.

"What is the meaning of this?" asked the king. The wisewoman replied, "Wear this ring always. Whatever happens, before you call it good or bad, touch the ring and read the inscription. That way, you will always be at peace."

If we practice slowing down and using our soothing rhythm breathing we are better able to access the wisdom of this ancient story. This story helps us remember that all things including difficult emotions, thoughts, and circumstances will pass.

If we look a little deeper at the fact that everything is impermanent we can start to see the importance and goodness of it. Impermanence makes it possible for pain to pass, for the beauty of the changing seasons, for sickness to be cured, for the acorn to grow into the oak tree, and for the child to grow up.

We can train ourselves to remember impermanence to help us live our values deeply each day and also to help us cope with painful experiences.

Impermanence is the way of the universe. Waking up to this truth can help us spend our lives in meaningful ways. We don't need to fear impermanence. We can actually learn to embrace impermanence over time, and in doing so we can see that it's sort of like a misunderstood person in our life who eventually becomes a great friend.

Sleep

"The woods are lovely, dark, and deep. But I have promises to keep, and miles to go before I sleep."

Robert Frost

When we are going for it and heading towards our valued path, we often are moving in such new territory that we may have trouble sleeping at times. (You may have trouble sleeping at times even when you're not going for it and are just on cruise control.) However, when we are really going for it we are heading outside our comfort zone and difficult thoughts and emotions will likely be showing up. As a reminder, humans were and are vulnerable when we go to sleep. Predators like lions, tigers, or bears could sneak up and attack at night in prehistoric times.

When you close your eyes at night, thoughts of the day show up and anticipations of tomorrow will often arise. Thoughts like:

- ✧ What did I forget to do today?
- ✧ That argument I had with my friend was awful! I'm still so mad!
- ✧ Why did I do that today? How could I be so stupid?

We may replay mistakes or events of the day over and over wishing we could have done something differently. And if all of that isn't enough, at a certain point we begin worrying about whether or not we will ever actually fall into sleep!

Sleep may sound like something we don't need to really worry about or pay attention to, but it is a big deal. When we become sleep-deprived our Threat (and protect) System gets triggered more easily. Our mind knows we are compromised and it needs to keep a lookout for danger at a higher level of intensity. When you are exhausted, the brain knows you could mistakenly walk out into the street in front of a moving car by accident.

All of us fall into this sleep trap at one time or another. So if you find yourself struggling to sleep, give yourself a break because it is normal to get caught in this struggle.

The sleep trap is when we begin to get anxious about not being able to sleep and then try really hard to fall asleep. The harder we try the more it activates our Threat System which says we are under attack and should not be sleeping right now. When we don't feel safe we are not designed to put our guard down and sleep.

The way out of the sleep trap doesn't look like the way out. The way out is to give up the goal of sleep. It's sort of like the wisdom of the archer who becomes frustrated because she can't seem to hit a bullseye. Her instructor who was watching tells her to let go of trying to hit the target and rather to just feel the tension of the string under her finger tips, feel the arrow's feathers against her cheek, and listen to the sound of the string as the arrow is released. (Essentially, the teacher is telling the archer to be mindfully aware in the present moment and detach from the outcome of the target.) The archer is surprised that in following these instructions she actually hits the bullseye!

PRACTICE #11:

Escaping the Sleep Trap = Deep Rest

Here is something really interesting: deep rest is almost as good as sleep because your body is not struggling and therefore it is able to renew itself, even without actual sleep. A former professor at Brown and the University of Texas Medical Schools and an internationally recognized expert on sleep, Dr. Matthew Edlund, talks about this in his book *The Power of Rest* and how we can tap into the healing power of rest. This isn't just a random fun fact—science tells us that this is true!

The way out of the sleep trap is a gradual process of learning how to let go of the goal of sleep and to instead aim for deep rest. Deep rest can be practiced by using our new brain's capacity for imagination. We can practice soothing rhythm breathing and then pull out our safe place imagery we worked on earlier in our Compassionate Other practice.

We can also practice bringing in the Compassionate Other and the Compassionate Self imagery to help us feel comforted and soothed.

You can use this practice whenever you are feeling stressed, but particularly when you are trying to rest deeply. Try it out during the day or as you are winding down in the evening before going to bed.

1. Start your slow soothing rhythm breathing. Remember slowing the breathing down slows the body and mind down.

2. What images give you a sense of safety and calmness? As you slow your breathing down and allow yourself to reflect, what people or animals give you a sense of safety, acceptance, and love?

3. Experiment with a calming touch. Try a hand on your belly and heart, or a hand upon your cheek, maybe even hug a pillow. As humans, we are soothed and calmed by touch and it can help us rest more deeply at night.

4. Now use your new brain's ability to imagine a person or a pet who loves you deeply telling you in a gentle voice to just rest, or if it is a pet, expressing this message through the look in their eyes. Imagine them saying or expressing nonverbally, "Just rest. Just rest," gently over and over again.

The mind is like a mischievous little monkey that is always jumping around grasping at all kinds of thoughts and emotions. However, the way out of the sleep trap is to employ the monkey mind by giving it the job to pay attention to your soothing rhythm breathing and to focus on this imagery. The monkey mind is not a good boss, but by giving it a job and making it our employee things go much better. You will find with practice that you will get better and better at escaping the sleep trap and that your monkey mind will become more cooperative and even helpful!

The Important Stuff

✧ We can use imagery to help move us towards what is most important to us in our lives. Imagery can bring our Soothing System online or it also can be used to activate our Drive System when we really need to take action on something we care about.

✧ The Compassionate Other is like a superhero's loyal sidekick that is there for you 100% of the time. We can use our new brain's capacity for imagination to bring our Compassionate Other out in full force. Research has shown that when we have a trusted friend with us we perceive challenges as less overwhelming. Even imagining that someone has our back calms us and gives us both strength and courage.

✧ The Compassionate Self is the superhero self we wear under our everyday clothes. It's the best version of ourselves. The four core qualities of our Compassionate Self are wisdom, caring-commitment, strength, and courage. We can create real brain changes— and changes in our lives—if we practice becoming our most compassionate version of ourselves.

✧ The wise Compassionate Self understands how our Threat System influences the thoughts and feelings we experience. The Compassionate Self helps us to remember to soothe and then encourages us to move in our valued direction.

✧ We can learn to train the compassionate part of our minds to be the captain of our ship. The Compassionate Self can calm down the difficult parts of ourselves that try to take over our lives.

✧ Everything in life is constantly changing. When we are heading towards our dreams and values it is helpful to remember this. The challenging moments, emotions, and thoughts all will pass as you move compassionately in your purpose-driven life.

✧ All of us fall into the sleep trap at one time or another. If you find yourself struggling to sleep, give yourself a break because it is normal to get caught in this struggle. The way out is to give up the goal of sleep.

For more resources, guided practices, and meditations, please visit our website:
www.MindfulCompassionForTeens.com.

"...Loving ourselves points us
to capacities of resilience,
compassion, and understanding
within that are simply part of
being alive."

Sharon Salzberg

Motivating with Kindness

chapter 7

"You have to learn to get up
from the table when love is
no longer being served."

Nina Simone

Why Is Love a Better Motivator than Shame?

We swim in a culture that sends us the message that we need to be
hard on ourselves and others if we want to reach our goals. Parents,
teachers, and coaches often hyperfocus on negatives. Teachers mark
the questions you got wrong on the test with an X through them.
Coaches often yell when players make mistakes and then take them
off the field. Parents are constantly pointing out a child's mistakes and
telling them what they did wrong.

These adults usually have good intentions but their approach is
often out of balance and their critical voice can easily become our
own inner critical voice when we make mistakes or struggle. These
points are backed up by the research of Dr. Kristen Neff. Dr. Neff
has found in her research that the biggest reason people aren't more
self-compassionate is that they are afraid—they have a real fear—
they will become lazy and self-indulgent (Neff, 2015). They believe
self-criticism is the answer because our culture says being hard on
ourselves is the only way we can achieve our goals or find success in
life.

As we spoke about earlier, this tricky brain of ours has a default mode of searching for the negative and then beating ourselves over the head with it in an attempt to try to keep us safe, correct our mistakes, and motivate us to improve. This is what we have been taught works and what our brain has evolved to do!

Just imagine that our prehistoric ancestor survives an attack of a dangerous animal and then afterwards that person plays the event over and over again in their mind to see if there is something they can learn. This review of the negative was important and served a purpose to help our prehistoric ancestor to be prepared for a future lethal attack. And you know what, in the present day this self-critical review may work in the short term, but it doesn't work in the long term. Over time, this inner critic begins to shame us with shoulds and should nots.

We become beaten down by our own inner critical voice, have difficulty trying new things, or even doing the things we love. With inner shaming we are unable to truly grow and flourish.

Let's look at something a little outside of ourselves as an example: Sculpting. It's probably not the first thing that jumps to your mind, but stick with us! Some sculptors work with marble and some work with clay. They are both trying to create something new and beautiful.

If you are the type of sculptor who works with a block of marble or stone, you are forced to use a chisel and a hammer. You must whack at this big block taking away large chunks and smaller chunks to achieve your goal. You may eventually be able to achieve the likeness or shape you imagine, but those cuts and whacks will always be a bit visible even if only in a small way. It is also a painful prospect for the the sculptor hitting the rock over and over, feeling the reverberation through the body.

Now let's look at a sculptor who works with clay. This artist isn't trying to force anything into submission by taking away, and cutting away large and small pieces (sometimes pieces that might be beautiful). This sculptor starts with a small lump and builds it up. This sculptor gently molds the clay and works it with her fingers and hands, adding more clay and shaping it to create the beauty she is seeking in the form she is trying to create.

If we bring this example back to us, think about how you would feel if someone was hitting you and trying to take pieces of you away to achieve a specific goal. This would feel terrible, harsh, and painful. And this would also activate our Threat System! Instead of lifting us up, it beats us down. If on the other hand, someone is lovingly and gently acknowledging what is already beautiful in us, creating a solid foundation and providing support and then adding to that, we would feel warmly encouraged.

You can mindfully choose the way of the clay sculptor for yourself.

PRACTICE #12

Looking at Our Threat-Detecting Mind

This practice illustrates how our threat-detecting mind works. Notice what shows up as you answer these questions.

What shows up in your mind when you fail at something that is important to you? What do you say to yourself?

Now imagine what you would you say to a dear friend who failed at something that was important to them?

Notice the difference between how we treat ourselves and a dear friend when we fail at something that is important.

Notice the difference in the tone of voice of how we would speak to a hurting friend as compared to the inner tone of voice we use with ourselves? Loving, harsh, gentle, supportive, kind, soothing, critical, belittling, shaming, understanding, etc...

What differences do you see?

When we take a step back and are able to mindfully observe how we might speak to a dear friend and ourselves, we are able then to choose how we want to show up as we move forward in our lives. It's a difficult shift and one that doesn't happen overnight or easily. But we can make the shift with continued practice.

"Remember that if you really want to motivate yourself, love is more powerful than fear."

Kristin Neff

How We Can Handle this Threat-Detecting Mind

Now that we have taken a look at our threat-detecting mind and how it operates, here are some practices we can use to handle this tricky brain of ours and motivate ourselves with love rather than shame or criticism.

"If you want others to be happy, practice compassion. If you want to be happy, practice compassion."

Dalai Lama

PRACTICE #13:

Compassionate Playlist

Our friend Dr. Laura Silberstein Tirch teaches teens in New York City to pull out their phones. She then has them look at all their music and carefully choose three songs that soothe them, support them, and generally give them the similar message or feeling as the letter from our Compassionate Self in Chapter 6. Laura says we can use the feelings cultivated by this music to help us start our day or soothe us in the middle of the day when we find ourselves dealing with difficulties and challenges.

From this place, we then can move towards what we want to achieve in our lives.

As you listen to the songs and feel your Compassionate Self coming through, you are actually bringing this Compassionate Self to life like an actor who is getting into character. Except you are not acting—this Compassionate Self is already within you waiting to be accessed. Remember you can always turn to these songs anytime day or night when you need a little support. And feel free to add to these songs as you come across more songs that soothe and uplift you.

Make a list of some of the songs you would like to add to your compassionate playlist. Why are you choosing each of these songs?

PRACTICE #14:

Bringing Your Future Self to the Present

Spend a few moments slowing down using your soothing rhythm breathing.

Now imagine watching a movie of your future self living your life and your dreams. See in vivid detail what you would be doing, how you would be going about your day, how you would be speaking to people, and even how you would carry your body. Imagine even the smallest details of the clothing you wear or your body posture. Next, imagine what words of support and wisdom this future self would give to your present self.

Even if you don't have a lot of time you can bring this future self imagery to your mind to help soothe and calm yourself. When you are short on time, take one or two slow deep breaths and gently bring back your future self image and its wisdom for five seconds. Notice how we can bring back this inner future self guide at moments when we need it.

We can use this touch-and-go skill anytime throughout our day at times of stress or at anytime we need guidance on what to do next in life. You don't need a long period of time to get in touch with your wise future self because it is always within you.

Practice #15:

Loving Kindness Meditation

The L word! No one in the world is more deserving of our love than ourselves.

There is all this talk about how you have to love yourself first before you can love someone else, but nobody tells us how to do it.

We all want the people we love and care for to have good things in their lives. If we break it down, we more specifically want them to be safe and protected, we want them to be mentally happy and content, we want them to be physically happy and well, and we want them to have peace in their lives.

However, we don't usually take time to think about these wishes for those we love and we especially don't take time to think about these wishes for ourselves. Because of the conditioning of shame in our culture and our tricky brain that defaults to find the negative, it can be helpful to practice what is called loving kindness meditation.

Let's first take a moment to slow down with our soothing rhythm breathing.

Now let's imagine some of the kind things you have done throughout your life. These can be small kindnesses that happen on a daily basis such as opening a door for someone, or giving someone a smile or a sincere compliment when it isn't necessary. Or it can be bigger things like helping a baby bird who was injured or being there for a friend who was going through a tough time. Just see these images in your mind in great detail.

You probably show loving kindness to others all the time whether you realize it or not. Now that we have awakened this capacity to care for others, we are going to intentionally send this out into the world and also direct it inward towards ourselves.

Sharon Salzberg is one of the leading teachers of loving kindness meditation in the United States. Sharon suggests that we start by sending loving kindness out into the world. Imagine a living being who brings a smile and a sense of warmth to you when you think of them. This could be a friend, a pet, a parent, or any living being you deeply care for. See this being in your mind's eye and gently say their name as you send the following wishes. Remember to say these slowly and really try to mindfully feel the meaning of each wish as you send it out. We are also going to coordinate saying these wishes with our breath. For example, breathing in and saying the words gently in your mind "may Heather be safe" and breathing out slowly saying "may Heather be happy." Let's give it a try!

May_____ be safe,
may_____ be happy,
may_____ be healthy, and
may_____ live with ease.

After sending out these wishes three times, imagine you are sitting or standing right next to the living being that just received your wishes. Imagine the two of you are surrounded by a warm light that holds and supports the both of you. You are in this warm space together and you are both feeling the loving kindness present in the space. As you imagine this, repeat these phrases of loving kindness and send these wishes to the both of you.

May we be safe,
may we be happy,
may we be healthy, and
may we live with ease.

Now imagine the that the image of the living being you have chosen gently starts to fade into the background and that you are now left standing in the warm light. Slowly recite these phrases for yourself with a loving tone of voice while placing a hand over your heart:

May I be safe,
may I be happy,
may I be healthy, and
may I live with ease.

Repeat these phrases three times or more. Please remember to listen to whatever feels good to you in the moment. If you feel you need more than three wishes of loving kindness for yourself then please go ahead and send them to yourself. On the other hand please also feel free to send the person or being you're sending these wishes to more wishes of loving kindness if that is what feels right.

Take a moment to notice how you felt in your body as you sent these loving wishes to another living being and then to yourself. For most of us this is very strange and different, but try to stay with it because this loving kindness practice is aimed to counter the negative bias of the mind that is hypercritical of us.

After you have finished this practice, make some observations (like a scientist) about how you are feeling. Pay close attention as you mindfully move through your day and your week. Notice how this loving kindness meditation may influence your life.

PRACTICE #16:

Where Are You in This Moment?

We can get so busy running around in our daily lives that many times we don't realize where we are or what we are doing.

How often do we end up in front of the refrigerator for the third time in an hour standing there with the door open wondering what we are doing there again?

How many times do we walk into a room and wonder why we've walked in there in the first place?

We all do things like this and the good news is that even with a quick check-in practice like this one, we can learn to be more present and mindfully aware in our daily lives.

Step 1: Sit or stand in a comfortable upright position.

Step 2: Stop and purposely bring your full attention to the soles of your feet. Wiggle your toes for a second if you need help focusing your attention.

Step 3: Notice what your hands and fingertips are touching. Relax your shoulders down, and take one long slow in breath to the count of five and breathe out to the count of ten.

Step 4: Ask yourself, "Am I doing what's important to me or do I gently need to choose a new course of action at this moment?"

Just like when you are driving somewhere, if you are lost in thought and miss a turn, you can always turn back around and start back in the direction you want to go. But the first thing we have to do is pause and check-in on where we are. We need to be present in order to even know if we missed the turn. Try taking this quick check in practice out on the road of life today and see if you can find three moments to use this practice. Be curious about what you notice!

Practice #17:

Becoming Your Compassionate Self

"All the world's a stage, and all the men and women merely players: they have their exits and their entrances; and (people) in (their lifetimes) play many parts..."

William Shakespeare

Most of the day we are living on autopilot. We wake up and we go through the motions of life not realizing that we actually have a choice. But what if we deliberately chose how we wanted to show up and the character or the role we wanted to play? What if we chose to play the role of the Compassionate Self?

The Compassionate Self is more than just an idea that we create in our mind. It's something we can actually do to help us take the controls back. We can wake up in the morning and purposely embody or become our Compassionate Self and then step into life with this purpose. And let's remember what that really means—

when we become our Compassionate Self we are
saying that we are becoming that highest version of
ourselves that sees the pain and suffering we and
others are experiencing, and we are committed to
do something to make things better.

What happens if we are on autopilot and don't explore the Compassionate Self?

Our tricky mind goes back into the default mode of searching the world for danger and inwardly scanning for personal flaws in ourselves. On the other hand, when we step into the Compassionate Self, it will support us, comfort us, encourage us, and help us tolerate any distress we encounter. The inner critical Threat (and protect) System is not going to be destroyed by the Compassionate Self, but rather comforted and calmed (This practice is inspired by the work of Dr. Dennis Tirch and Dr. Paul Gilbert.)

Step 1: Please allow your eyes to soften and begin to slow your breathing. Breathe in through the nose for the count of five and out through your mouth for the count of five. As you breathe out mentally whisper to yourself "slowing down, slowing down, slowing down."

Step 2: Imagine a version of yourself that is kind, confident, and wise. Take in all of the details of this compassionate version of yourself. Look at the health in the eyes, in the skin, and in the body. Notice the clothes that you would be wearing and even your body posture. Imagine that this part of you is 100% committed to your well-being and will always have your back.

Step 3: Take a moment to imagine how that Compassionate Self lives in the world. See a movie in your mind of how your Compassionate Self would live. As you watch the Compassionate Self, notice how they would greet people, and even how they carry their body when they walk. Hear the kind, confident, loving voice of your Compassionate Self in your mind.

Step 4: Now allow yourself to refocus your eyes and stand. Imagine that you're giving your Compassionate Self a hug. Reach out with your arms wide open and imagine that you're hugging your Compassionate Self. As you lean in and hug, your Compassionate Self actually absorbs into your body and you can feel this inner strength, calmness, wisdom, and maturity flowing throughout your body.

Step 5: Feeling the Compassionate Self from the inside out, walk around the room as if you are this compassionate part of you right now. As you walk, imagine yourself greeting a friend, giving them a hug or looking them in the eyes and saying hello.

Step 6: Finally, imagine that you're doing a daily task like brushing your teeth, washing your face, putting your clothes on, or even greeting the family dog or cat as your Compassionate Self. Notice how you feel in your body. Maybe you move more fluidly and easily or maybe you even have a smile on your face. You may become aware that you feel stronger and maybe you're standing up taller. You even may notice yourself feeling more energetic and in less physical pain.

This practice allows you to actually try on the Compassionate Self for a few moments. It shows you how it feels and that it is possible to become more compassionate towards yourself and others purposely throughout the day.

There is a wonderful researcher, Dr. Marcela Matos in Portugal, whose research focuses on this. Marcela is researching how powerful it is to have people actually practice becoming their compassionate selves as if they're actors getting into a role for a play. Her research shows that people experience less anxiety, depression, and rage when they practice becoming their compassionate selves literally off and on throughout the day.

If you're willing, experiment with purposely slowing down and mindfully practicing becoming your Compassionate Self throughout your day. At first, start small with just two to three minutes, three times a day. Gradually, you can increase your time to five minutes or longer, three times a day. Nobody will know you're doing this unless you tell them. However, they may notice you being more confident, calm, engaged, and generally more relaxed and happy.

PRACTICE #18

You Have Always Been Enough

No one is achieving all the time.

No one is living their values perfectly everyday.

No one has a life free of mistakes. No one has relationships that are perfect and loving all the time.

And even with all of these acknowledgments, we are still enough!

Ask your dog or cat what they are striving for and if they feel like they are enough. This is a silly question, but let's think about the answer. Animals don't get grades or an income but we wouldn't say they are worthless or not enough.

We are already enough just as we are regardless of what our mind's inner critic may say. We can learn to stop and rest in our enoughness. Where are you when you are asleep? You aren't achieving or doing anything, you're just asleep and you are still enough just as you are. We can learn to take time outs in the game of life to stop and rest in enoughness. Resting in enoughness is a practice we can lovingly tune into again and again.

Resting in "I Am Enough" Meditation:

✧ Begin with your soothing rhythm breathing. Purposely slowing down the breath and finding your warm friendly facial expression.

✧ Bring your attention to the soles of your feet and notice the sensation in your feet. (Wiggle your toes for a second or two if you need help noticing the feet.)

✧ Now bring your attention to your hands. Become aware of the sensations in your hands and notice what your fingertips are touching.

✧ When you feel grounded and ready, bring your full attention to your in breath and as you breathe in say to yourself with a supportive inner voice the words, "I AM ENOUGH."

✧ Then as you exhale slowly and smoothly say gently to yourself, "JUST AS I AM."

You may want to place a hand on your heart or on your cheek as you repeat these phrases as you breathe in and out. If you're at a desk you can even place a hand on your stomach so no one can see your soothing gesture.

Repeat these phrases as many times as you need. Some days you may need more and some days you may need less. This practice is very flexible and can be used throughout your day as often as you need it because you don't necessarily have to close your eyes to do this practice.

Your inner critic may show up when you first start using this practice (and often it does show up). It might say something like,

"No you're not enough just as you are."

If this happens, let's try something a little different. Surprise your inner critic by smiling with the calm wise smile of our Compassionate Self. Then say inwardly,

"I know you are only trying to help, but we are not stopping and we are going to breathe like this and say these phrases whether you agree or not."

The inner critic may stay around for awhile like a yappy dog that never bites. After awhile, though, the inner critic will start to become bored when it notices you're not avoiding it or reacting to it with aggression. It will lose interest as you calmly continue what you are doing. Your commitment to knowing you are enough (and that you have always been enough) will open up possibility and potential before you and will allow you to see options where none existed before. When you know you are enough, you have all that you need in that moment.

After completing this practice, doodle or draw whatever shows up for you. Let yourself be free to create, whether it is abstract or concrete and specific. Whatever shows up is enough.

"Sometimes you have to stand up for yourself, to yourself."

Atticus

PRACTICE #19:

Mindful Walking

This human body we have is changing all the time throughout our entire lives, but most rapidly when we are babies and when we are adolescents and teens. Sometimes when we don't like what is going on with our bodies we tend to want to hide.

If there is something you are struggling with in relation to your body—whether you think you are not thin enough, or too thin, or if you are frustrated with the acne that shows up regardless of what you do to prevent it—instinctively you might slouch your shoulders or look down when talking to people so they don't fully see you. This natural instinct to hide, although it might feel like a solution in the short term, actually makes things worse.

By looking down and slouching we send a message to our bodies that we are under attack. If you watch a turtle under attack it will pull into its shell. We often do the same thing without realizing it. The body holds tension as if it is being attacked when our inner critic shows up or when we are in stressful situations.

Luckily there is a remedy we can learn to apply when we notice ourselves pulling into our shell: mindful walking while adopting the posture of our Compassionate Self.

Mindful walking can help bring us back to the present moment and help us release these stressful situations as well as fear and tension, shifting us out of the Threat System.

As you slow down your breathing and take on the body posture of your Compassionate Self it sends a message to the body that you are not actually under attack. The Compassionate Self stands in an upright, confident, and calm posture with a slight smile. This posture also makes it easier for your body to breathe with your shoulders, back, and head up.

You may be wondering how mindful walking is different from the walking you do every day. After all, you are still moving your arms and legs and going from point A to point B. However, in mindful walking your goal is not to move from point A to point B—that's just the by-product. Your goal is to arrive in the present moment with each step.

In mindful walking you are moving your body through space with full awareness and attention on the present moment.

At first, this may seem a little strange or challenging and so it is helpful to have some guidelines.

1. Choose where you will walk. Start with a short distance, for example from the car to your front door or simply across a room.
2. As you begin to walk, bring your awareness to your body. There is no right or wrong way to practice mindful walking.

Bring your full attention to the soles of your feet.

Notice the sensations of your feet making contact with the ground. Coordinate your breath with the movement of your feet and body. Breathing in, take a few steps forward and count your footsteps with your in-breath. Breathing out, exhale and again count your footsteps with the out-breath. Often we find that when we begin this practice it's easiest to start with an inhale of four to five counts/footsteps and an exhale of six to eight counts/footsteps; however, listen to your body and experiment with what feels best to you and your breathing.

3. Once you feel a bit more comfortable with walking in this way, remember to bring in your Compassionate Self body posture if you aren't already practicing this. Walk with your shoulders back and head up but relaxed, embodying your calm and confident self with a slight smile on your face.

What do you notice as you practice this mindful way of walking as your Compassionate Self?

Regardless of your pace and speed, the main objective is to be mindful and aware of your body and your movement in the present moment. This may feel awkward at first, but if you can take one step like this then you can take two. You're not trying to get anywhere. You are just arriving in the present moment with each step.

These gentle and repeated movements teach us how to bring our mind back to our bodies and out of the spinning, self-critical thoughts we have at times.

Walking and moving our bodies in this way is a form of mindfulness meditation and can be very helpful for those who find traditional sitting meditations more challenging. Experiment with placing your attention on your movement, and your breath, and your surroundings. If you notice your mind wandering, gently bring it back to your mindful walking and your breath.

You can do mindful walking anywhere and any time that you walk from one spot to another. It's not something that looks funny or strange while you are doing it. From the outside, it just looks like you are walking. No one will know that you are practicing mindful walking. To everyone who might be looking, you are just walking naturally (while secretly coordinating your breathing and your steps).

The Important Stuff

✧ We swim in a culture that sends us the message that we need to be hard on ourselves and others if we want to reach our goals. This tricky brain of ours has a default mode of searching for the negative and then beating ourselves over the head with it in an attempt to try to keep us safe, correct our mistakes, and motivate us to improve. This is what we have been taught works and what our brain has evolved to do!

✧ This review of the negative was critical to help our prehistoric ancestors to be prepared for an attack. In the present day, this self-critical review may work in the short term, but doesn't work in the long term. With inner shaming we are unable to truly grow and flourish.

✧ Motivating with kindness—lovingly and gently acknowledging what is already beautiful in us—creates a solid foundation and provides support and encouragement.

✧ Compassionate practices help us handle this tricky brain of ours and motivate ourselves with love and kindness rather than shame or criticism. Some of these compassionate practices that can be very handy in dealing with this tricky brain of ours include:

  • creating a compassionate playlist on your phone,
  • bringing your future self to the present moment,
  • a loving kindness meditation for yourself and others,
  • tapping into what is happening right now in this moment,
  • recognizing that you are enough, and
  • mindful walking to reduce stress and body tension.

For more resources, guided practices, and meditations, please visit our website: www.MindfulCompassionForTeens.com.

"Love doesn't just sit there, like a stone, it has to be made, like bread; remade all the time, made new."

Ursula K. Le Guin

chapter

7

What Else Can I Do?

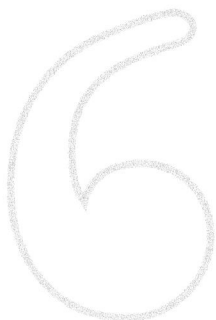

"Kindness is a language that
the blind can see and the deaf
can hear."

Mark Twain

Being There for All Parts of Yourself

Do you ever feel like you have different parts of yourself? We've been
talking a lot about how to bring your Compassionate Self out or how to
become your Compassionate Self, but as you have probably felt, we have
a lot going on in this mind of ours. Sometimes a different you shows up
out of nowhere, right? It happens to all of us. One minute you're this calm
relaxed self and then the next minute you're this angry or anxious self. This
often leaves you wondering,

"Where did that part of me
come from?"

Well the truth is we are really made up of multiple selves and there's
nothing wrong with us when these different parts of us randomly show up
(Irons, 2018).

Just because it seems like these different parts
of us randomly show up, though, doesn't mean we
have to follow their lead all the time.

We don't need to be pushed around by these parts of ourselves that pop up and often hijack our lives. We can be there for them, but not have them be the boss and run the show.

It is possible to purposely and mindfully nurture a different part of yourself that can be like the director of this cast of characters within us. Or if you don't like the idea of a director and a cast of characters, how about a captain of a ship in charge of a large crew as our friend Dr. Russell Kolts talks about in his book *CFT Made Simple*? Either way, you get the idea.

> You can nurture a self to be in charge and you don't have to be dragged around by these multiple selves that seem to show up unexpectedly.

By developing and nurturing this Compassionate Self, we can purposely train this part of us to be the director of the movie of our lives. As we have all heard, some actors are more challenging to work with than others. A good director has the skill to keep the cast and crew going even when one of them starts creating difficulties on the set. A good director is there for all of the actors and can calm down even the most challenging ones.

Nurturing Your Compassionate Self

PRACTICE #20:

Your Best Self—Building Your Character

Imagine your highest and best version of yourself as a character in a movie or a video game. This character would have all the character traits that you desire. You may want to think about yourself at your best or about people you admire and the traits they share. Don't worry about whether or not you have these traits right now. Just have fun building this character. List all of the traits of your character. Here are some examples to get you started:

Playful, kind, confident, wise, open-minded, peaceful, patient, understanding, strong, brave, sincere, persevering, forgiving.

If you like, you can also describe how this character would behave in certain situations, how they would interact with different people, etc. There's no limit on what this character does. Allow yourself to take your time and really explore. And if writing doesn't feel good to you as you express these ideas, feel free to draw or doodle.

PRACTICE #21:

The Gift of the Compassionate-Self Meditation

To begin, allow yourself to slow down and become balanced by using your soothing rhythm breathing. Take your time.

There is no race that we have to complete. We are often in a wound up threat-detection mode and it takes a little time to send our body this slow-down message through our breathing. If we rush too quickly to our imagery work we will struggle because our mind will be wanting to scan for danger and will also be looking for problems to solve.

After about two minutes of soothing rhythm breathing, imagine your Compassionate Self—that highest and best self within you. What if your Compassionate Self were to give you a special gift to remind you of what it wants you to remember or know? Imagine what that would be. This could be something small that symbolizes support and wisdom. This symbol could be something that is placed into your hand or in a pocket or a purse and could be pulled out whenever you need it.

If you are struggling to imagine this symbolic gift, that's OK! Just take your time.

You may want to imagine that you can hold up this gift to the light so that you can see it more clearly. The gift could be something from nature or something created like a coin or a heart.

Notice in your mind's eye the color, shape, weight, and texture. Also look closely to notice if there is anything written on it or if there is artwork of any sort on it. Make a high-definition recording of this gift in your mind and bring this memory back with you the best that you can. It's okay if your gift is not totally clear in your mind's eye because it is more important to just have a sense of the warm, supportive feeling it represents to you.

Next, imagine that you have this gift from your Compassionate Self in your hand right at this very moment. Where would you keep this gift if you wanted to keep it with you throughout your day? For example, you may want to keep it on a chain and wear it around your neck, or you may want to keep it in your shirt pocket close to your heart, or in a pants pocket next to your phone.

Imagine now that you are actually placing this compassionate gift in that special place you imagined in your mind's eye. Throughout your day when you are feeling stressed or when difficult thoughts and emotions are showing up, turn to this compassionate gift. Think of it as if it was a kind of anchor that could ground you and give strength in that difficult moment. Make physical contact with your imagined gift in some way. If you imagined this gift resting in your pocket, tap or put your hand in your pocket. If you imagined this gift on a necklace, place your hand on your chest over where a necklace might rest.

No one around you will know what you are doing and you will be able to turn to this gift any time of day or night.

Many athletes and musicians have reminders that they bring with them to give them inner strength when they go out to perform. Some athletes put the initials of someone they love on their shoes or in the back of their hat. Some musicians wear a bracelet or special piece of clothing that represents strength or reminds them of a supportive other who loves them. Athletes and musicians have routines of taking these things purposely with them when they go out on the field or up on stage. We can always bring our Compassionate Self's gift with us when we go out onto the metaphorical playing field or stage of our lives.

What gift did your Compassionate Self give you? Where will you keep it how will it serve as a reminder for you of strength and support?

PRACTICE #22:

Mindful Doodle

Art can be a very mindful and purposeful practice to help us connect with our Compassionate Self. The problem is that sometimes we don't allow ourselves the space to just let go without judgment or criticism. But... what if you did? What if you allowed yourself to just doodle for a bit on the page?

Get out some markers, colored pencils, pens—whatever you like—and set your marker, pencil, or pen on the paper and just let whatever comes out flow. Before you begin, bring your Compassionate Self to your mind's eye.

Notice the colors, shapes, and the feelings of warmth and encouragement that show up. Allow all of it to fill the page.

Now, notice what colors showed up in your doodle.

Does a certain color represent compassion to you? What did you notice about your mind as you were drawing? Was it quiet or active with lots of thoughts? What symbols or designs in your doodle mean something to you?

Take a picture of this mindful doodle on your phone so you can have it with you at any time you might need it during the day or night.

PRACTICE #23:

Theme Song

Remember when we were imagining earlier that we were a character or an actor in a movie? Let's bring that image back again. Now, have you noticed when you are watching a movie that often different characters have a theme song when they come into a scene or as they are entering a room? What would your Compassionate Self's theme music be walking into that first scene (or every scene for that matter) of the movie of your life?

> What would play in the background as your Compassionate Self walks into a room?

Take a look right now at the music on your phone and use your imagination as you listen to potential songs that would be your Compassionate Self's theme music. Try out a few songs and see which ones feel like the best fit.

Coming Back into Alignment the Compassionate Way

At times after cars get into accidents, the front and back tires will become out of alignment. In fact, sometimes the front and back tires can get out out of alignment just from regular wear and tear every day on the roads. We hit a pothole or travel over a rough road and sometimes that's all it takes! When this happens, the car goes down the road and it looks odd because the back tires aren't aligned with the front. But it doesn't just look odd, the car is harder to steer when the wheels are out of alignment and the tires wear unevenly which makes it unsafe to drive the car after a while.

Our minds also get out of alignment with our body when we experience emotional crashes or situations. We have a conflict with someone and we replay the argument in our mind over and over again, firing up our Threat System. Then a bit later we notice that our jaw aches because we must have been clenching it, or our lower back aches because we were tensing those muscles tightly as if we we were getting ready to prepare ourselves to fight or run away.

What can we do when this happens? A body scan exercise can be used at any place and at any time to help us mindfully identify where we are out of alignment and then bring us back into alignment.

You always have your body with you so this is a good practice to keep on hand.

PRACTICE #24:

Body Scan

Start with your slow rhythm breathing. After about two minutes, with your eyes closed let's bring to mind something that is a little or mildly upsetting. Just remember that situation or the subject that was upsetting.

Now gently bring your attention to your body and notice what physical sensations are showing up. See if you can bring your full attention to them and name their quality, such as:

⬥ tightness in my chest,

⬥ tingly feeling in my fingers,

⬥ warmth around my eyes, and so on.

Now, see if you can say hello to these sensations. Breathe into these sensations of tightness or whatever else might be showing up and say,

"I allow you to be here."

With your next in breath and out breath, send that place of tension or stress a feeling of warmth, love, and healing. Sometimes it helps to imagine a color or a light moving to this spot in your body, such as a healing green light, a pink or rose colored light or a white light.

What do you notice after allowing this in your body and then sending it some loving kindness?

> When we get stressed, our attention goes away from our body up into our head with all of its relentless thoughts. Bringing our attention to our body anchors us when storms of emotion show up in our lives.

As a sophomore in high school I (Chris) had severe lower back pain. My parents took me to a sports medicine doctor who told me that my muscles were so tight that they were pulling on my lower back. What they weren't aware of was how my inner Threat System was being triggered all day long in school where I didn't get any help with my dyslexia, learning disability, and ADHD. As a result my inner critic would attack me with critical thoughts and then my body would tense up as if I was actually preparing to physically defend myself.

This experience helped me later in life to better understand and help a teenage client who said her back was severely hurting. Like me, she struggled with ADHD symptoms. I asked her how the back pain was on Saturdays. She was surprised as she reflected that her back pain was actually not that bad at all on Saturdays. We worked together on practicing the body scan and combined it with some gentle movement (walking and gentle stretches). Overtime her back pain was transformed and she knew how to handle it when it began to tighten up again.

Noticing body tension, and then breathing into that area, and then allowing it to be there. By doing this we are bringing a soft and gentle attention to our body discomfort and soothing it, instead of ignoring it and getting pulled back up into our heads.

We are taking back our power.

Notice any little changes in these sensations as you practice this. Maybe you feel tension softening or releasing. Maybe you feel a sensation changing from coolness to warmth. There is no right or wrong. Just bring awareness to the present moment and notice what happens.

PRACTICE #25:

Sitting Down in the Eye of the Storm

In our life storms seem to pop up out of nowhere. Unwanted situations happen, and along with these situations come the storms of challenging thoughts and emotions; it's easy to feel as if you are being swept away by them. When we get swept away in the storm we have a hard time seeing our way forward and moving in our valued direction. However, in every storm there is a still calm place in the very center which people call the eye of the storm.

Finding this still calm place can be a practice.

A great way to practice finding and resting in this calm eye of the storm is the exercise of slowing down with our soothing rhythm breathing and then bringing our attention to what physical sensations are showing up in the body.

You can start to find the still place by mindfully coming back to the present moment and your physical senses.

✧ Starting with your ears, notice what sounds are available at that moment.

✧ Moving to your eyes, notice three objects around you and all of their details: color, shape, interesting marks, ridges, etc.

✧ Notice with your body three things you can feel: feet pressing against the floor, your hand touching this book, your back pressing against your chair, etc.

This simple task accompanied by your soothing rhythm breathing will bring you into the still place and out of the storm of difficult thoughts and emotions so you can get your bearings and start out again in your valued direction.

PRACTICE #26:

Dealing with Distractions

Distractions. Our world is full of them. And if that isn't enough, sometimes our mind will create them for us even when we are engaged in something important and meaningful.

Whether you are trying to complete your homework, a project, or practice a piece of music or a sport, distractions—like social media, texting, interruptions from friends and family, loud noises in your neighborhood, YouTube, the list could go on and on—will most definitely show up and attempt to take your attention away!

How can we deal with this distraction then? As we know, in our world distractions are all around us and they will always be there. We need to learn to see the distraction and then bring ourselves back to the task at hand—especially if it is a task that is aligned with our values and our valued path in life.

Step 1: Notice you're distracted.
Awareness: "Oh, I'm day dreaming." Or "Why are they talking so loud?"

Step 2: Bring your attention to your breath, or the soles of your feet. This might take a bit, but with practice it will become easier.

Focusing on your breath or on the soles of your feet is grounding and creates an anchor to pull your attention back to this moment.

Step 3: Forgive yourself for being distracted and remember that being distracted is part of having a human brain.

The human brain is always scanning the environment for what other things are going on in the attempt to keep us safe. In primitive times when people had to hunt daily for food, a bored hunter was a dead hunter. A bored hunter, who was not paying attention to the surroundings, scanning for danger, or looking for food, wouldn't live very long. Our minds are designed and have evolved to do this.

Step 4: Come back to your intention for completing the task and your values.

Why is this task important?

How is it helping you to move along on your valued path?

It's hard to persevere on tasks that don't appear to have personal meaning to us so that's why it's helpful to regularly remind ourselves of these things.

Step 5: Start again by bringing your Compassionate Self into the game.

Use some encouraging statements like:
"I've got this!"

"I'm making progress one small step at a time."

"Everyone has distractions that pop up. I can continue even with these distractions and over time I will achieve my goal."

The Important Stuff

✧ We have a lot going on in this mind of ours. Sometimes a different you shows up out of nowhere. There is nothing wrong with us when these different parts of us randomly show up; however, we don't need to be ruled by this cast of characters.

✧ It is possible to purposely nurture a different part of yourself that can be like the director of this cast of characters within us. We can nurture a Compassionate Self to be in charge and we don't have to be dragged around by the multiple selves that seem to show up unexpectedly and sometimes hijack our lives. We outlined six practices in this chapter to help nurture that Compassionate Self within us:

- Your Best Self: Building Your Character
- The Gift of Compassionate-Self Meditation
- Mindful Doodle
- Theme Song

✧ With all of the stress we experience every day, we can easily get out of alignment with our minds and bodies. When this happens we may feel physical pain or tension in the body, find it more difficult to stay calm, to soothe ourselves, and to do the things that are truly important to us. A few simple practices can make all the difference when we want to come back to our mind/body alignment:

- Body Scan
- Sitting Down in the Eye of the Storm
- Dealing with Distractions

For more resources, guided practices, and meditations, please visit our website: www.MindfulCompassionForTeens.com.

"Minds are like parachutes—
they only function when open."

Thomas Dewar

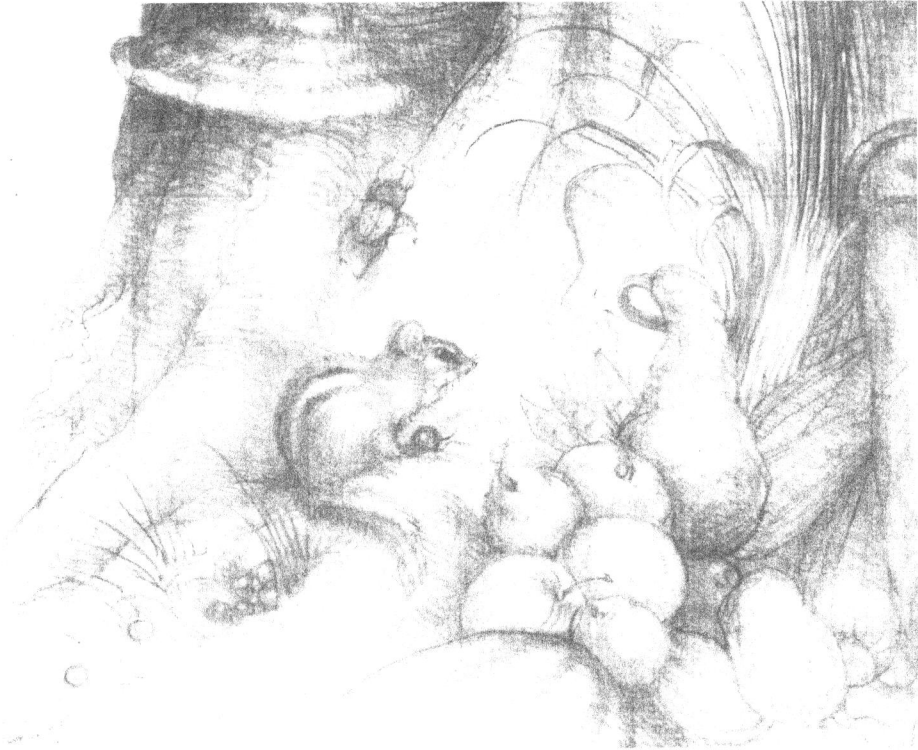

What Else Can I Do?

chapter 9

Following the Spark

"The future is totally open, and we are writing it moment to moment."

Pema Chodron

Your Gifts and Strengths Lead the Way

We don't become successful and contented by doing what we stink at or by focusing on what we don't like! We become successful and contented by discovering our strengths and using them as much as possible in our daily lives. However, sometimes our society and our schools send a message that if you're not smart in every subject then you're not intelligent or you're not going to be able to make it in the world. They tend to encourage us to overfocus on the areas where we struggle and not on our strengths.

Notice what your mind says when you try to answer these questions:

What are my strengths? What do I love? What comes easily and naturally to me in life?

You may notice that your mind becomes confused or critical. You may be thinking, "I have no idea!" Or you may have thoughts like, "I'm not that good at anything," or "I don't want to write this down because maybe it is not true."

We used to live in very small communities where each child's unique gifts were identified, honored, and fostered by the entire group. You would then contribute to the group by becoming the next healer, hunter, clothing maker, animal caretaker, chef, builder, storyteller, musician, artist, historian, organizer, comedian-jester, etc. In the modern world, we are often heavily influenced to ignore our gifts and choose a career that has the potential to make money even if it has nothing to do with our gifts or what we feel called to do.

If you feel like you don't know what your strengths are, that's okay! You may want to think about the things you do where you feel a sense of joy, accomplishment, or pride. These things may be challenging for you, but even in the challenge you are having fun or enjoying the process. In fact, an element of challenge that feels good is a sure sign that you are on the right path.

Think back on your past and take a good look at the things that come more naturally for you, things that you love, things that bring you joy. There is truth here—sometimes you may have to dig a little to get to the core aspect of what that is. And if you are unsure, try some things out! Write a poem or short story, do some challenging math problems, conduct your own experiment, sketch a design for some new fashion or furniture or a building, plant some flowers, build a shelf—just try something that is intriguing to you!

Our gifts and our strengths are like a spark that can fire up our inspiration!

It's helpful to remember that all it takes is the smallest of sparks to create the largest fire. This spark can give us the courage to go for what is really important to us and help us tolerate the discomfort that we will inevitably encounter on this path.

People can take away your cars, homes, TVs, computers, or phones, but they can't take away your strengths and gifts. Many people climb a career ladder for years and then realize after they've climbed to the top (or sometimes halfway up) that this ladder they've been climbing is up against the wrong wall. This is no fault of their own! Our society pushes people to stop listening to those things that bring them joy and to the things that are their true strengths.

Many modern societies are cutting young people off from their innate gifts by forcing them to learn in ways that don't necessarily utilize their natural inborn gifts, strengths, and abilities. Often, children are made to study in school by sitting in rows, staying quiet, learning mostly auditorily, and the curriculum is not tailored to their individual interests or abilities. Many young people grow up thinking they are dumb because of this way of teaching. For many people, this is comparable to asking a fish to climb a tree.

Albert Einstein wrote,

> "Everybody is a genius. But if you judge a fish by its ability to climb a tree, it will live its whole life believing that it is stupid."

This concept of identifying your strengths and what brings you joy is very ancient. We find this concept in one of the oldest written languages in the world, Sanskrit. The message in Sanskrit is written as "sat, chit, ananda" which means "true being, true consciousness, and true bliss." So this means that by identifying your joy or "bliss" (and following it), you will come to your true being and then true awareness will follow.

This may seem a bit out there, but it lets us know that this idea has been around for thousands of years. In recent times the researcher Dr. Martin Seligman at the University of Pennsylvania has shown scientifically that people who identify their strengths and utilize them frequently in their lives have greater well-being and happiness.

Your superpowers (strengths) have always been there.

Making Fish Climb Trees

In the United States we often demoralize children and cut them off from their inborn gifts through our education system. Then these children become adults and are encouraged to take high-status jobs that may have nothing to do with the gifts they were born with or those that they have cultivated over time through their interests and strengths.

Sometimes teens become bombarded by the thought,

"If I can't make it here in school, how will I ever make it in the real world?"

And it's not surprising that this is the thought that takes over—it's what adults are telling them day after day. Here's the thing:

there are no stupid people and we all have gifts to offer and to contribute to this world. We can reconnect with our gifts and let go of what our society and in turn what our own mind says is possible for us!

High school is just the beginning. Often you hear adults say something like,

"High school should be the best time of your life!" or "High school was the best time of my life!"

We're here to break it down a bit for you—high school is four years. That's it. The average lifetime is 75+ years. It's just the beginning of your exploration and journey in life.

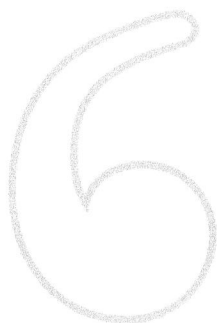

"Whatever you can do, or dream you can do, begin it. Boldness has genius, power, and magic in it. Begin it now."

Goethe

With our Compassionate Self and Compassionate Other at our side, we can allow ourselves to explore. This may mean that we have success, but also that we allow ourselves to falter and then begin again and again in our pursuit of our valued life direction, dreams, and goals.

We can let go of unworkable thoughts and soothe difficult emotions as we pursue our life's greatest work. We can use our innate gifts and strengths!

Harriet Tubman, Albert Einstein, Gandhi, Susan B. Anthony, Michael Jordan, Louisa May Alcott, Anne Morrow Lindbergh, Jesse Owens, and many, many more famous people all struggled in school and in life as teens. They each discovered the things that brought joy and meaning to their lives. They allowed their true gifts to come forth and explored what was truly important to them. By constantly keeping their values in mind and utilizing their gifts, each of these now famous people were able to achieve amazing things that other people did not think possible for them when they were teens.

Slowing Down

We live in a society that highly praises productivity and we often hear the words "don't waste time" or "time is money." The problem? This is a trap!

The more we get worn down by trying to be always productive, the more our minds become taken over by the Threat System. We will make more mistakes, get into more conflicts with others, and in general we will struggle more with the threat emotions of fear, anger, and sadness.

Embrace the concept that rest, recovery, and reflection are essential parts of the progress towards a successful and happy life."

Zach Galifianakis

An alternative is that we can learn to pursue our dream or our spark through soothing ourselves and then *enlisting* our Drive System by consistently taking small, purposeful steps. The way you eat an elephant is one bite at a time. Or if you are a vegetarian, the way you eat an elephant-sized tomato is one bite at a time! When we do things this way, our minds and our bodies will respond with a sense of ease. Ultimately, we will be more creative when we don't feel like we are under tremendous threat.

As Zen Master Thich Nhat Hanh (a global spiritual leader, poet, and peace activist) says, it takes a bit of practice to break free from the habit energy of rushing and always pushing hard to make progress. This habit energy comes from our primitive ancestors and even our not-so-long-ago ancestors who had to be in constant motion to survive. This can be challenging to learn to slow down, but you can do it!

When we learn to slow down we become more compassionate, creative, curious, and calm. There are many old sayings that remind us of the importance of taking small purposeful steps and of the wisdom that small things can make a big difference:

✧ The ten-story building arose from one lump of clay.
✧ The journey of a thousand miles begins with one step.
✧ A large oak tree grows from a tiny acorn.
✧ A small ray of light can penetrate even the deepest darkness.

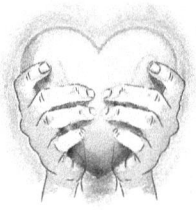

PRACTICE #27:

Soothing and Then Moving

When you feel yourself drifting off your path or you are overwhelmed by the bigness of what is in front of you, slowing down is one of the most important things you can do to speed up. And to slow down, we need to see where we are in the present moment and also soothe that Threat System that we know so well.

- ✧ Notice where you are and what is around you: Stop right now and find three objects in the room with your eyes.

- ✧ Allow curiosity to take over: Become really curious about your three objects. Why are they here? Notice the shape, color, texture of these objects.

- ✧ Breathe: Close your eyes for three slow deep breaths. (As we slow down, we ground ourselves and are able to see more clearly what is most important to us in that moment.) Now begin back to the task at hand or stop what you are doing and change direction. You may also realize after slowing down that what you truly need is just time to rest for a moment rather than taking action in any direction. Once you have taken the time to recharge, you can then continue on your valued path with renewed energy and focus.

Remembering You Can Always Start Again

It's so easy to forget that we can always start again. No matter how many times we fall down we can always stand up and begin again from where we are.

But, there is a difference between just starting again and starting again with compassionate encouragement. As we develop our compassionate minds, we can get better and better at helping ourselves get back up with compassionate encouragement rather than harsh self-criticism when we have a setback or a perceived failure.

Just imagine a child learning to walk and how many times they fall down before they actually learn to walk. By training our compassionate mind skills we will have the ability to encourage ourselves to get back up again and again, no matter how many times we stumble.

You may remember the metaphor we talked about in Chapter 7 (Motivating with Kindness) about the different ways an artist can attempt to create a beautiful sculpture. The Compassionate Self uses the powerful approach of being like an artist creating a sculpture out of clay. The inner critic is the artist with a hammer and a chisel in front of a block of marble.

The Compassionate Self builds us up like a sculptor with clay, adding on to the creation and enhancing it with each new lump of clay. The inner critic with a block of marble whacks away at the marble, trying to shape it and make it into something beautiful. What happens is that the hits of the hammer and chisel hurt us so very much that over time we become beaten down and demoralized by this approach. This hammer and chisel approach is instinctive. We hit ourselves with self-criticism, not realizing that this is ineffective for creating change and living a fulfilled life.

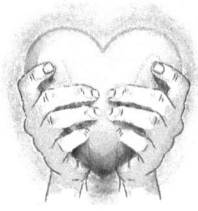

PRACTICE #28:

Starting Again After Setbacks

Let's see what happens when we allow little setbacks to be part of the plan and the way that we walk through life.

⬥ Stand in your Compassionate Self body posture and slow your breathing down with your slow rhythm breathing.

⬥ Gently tell yourself in a supportive kind voice, "Mistakes happen. Mistakes are expected. Just start again. Gently, start again."

⬥ Allow yourself to create a warm and friendly facial expression as if you're meeting a good friend. Then, start again on whatever tasks or situation you're dealing with.

It doesn't matter how many times in life we need to start again. As we continue to practice using compassionate encouragement we will see that these mistakes are really places of great learning and discovery. Your Compassionate Self will become stronger and will be able to tolerate the distress of these mistakes or perceived setbacks. We will then be able to learn and self-correct much faster. We will also gradually become more patient and loving to those around us as a result of this inner work.

All human beings on this planet could benefit from this practice. As you get better at this practice you will notice your friends, family members, and people in the community around you falling into this inner-critical trap and then struggling to start again.

Over time you will have more compassion for them. You may even become an inspiration through this new way you are living. Believe it or not, your friends may even ask you for help when they are struggling. Changes like the ones you are making do not go unnoticed (even if people don't say anything to you about it). Positive changes in you will be coming through even though your friends and others may not know what is different.

You are becoming more resilient
as you get better and better at
living in this new way!

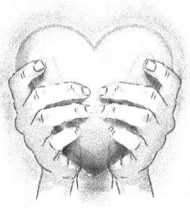

PRACTICE #29:

Quick Restart

Sometimes it's helpful to have a physical restart ritual. College and professional sports teams have rituals to help them get back into the game quickly and let go of mistakes so that they can start performing at a high level again. Teams usually come up with a start again ritual that everyone can agree upon and that is helpful for them.

Colorado State's men's basketball team chose a quick two taps over their heart after a mistake and then would mentally tell themselves "That's OK—next play." The next play is the most important play in the game. The two physical taps let them come back to the present moment and out of their heads and back into the game. You can create your own mistake ritual that can help you gently start again with compassionate courage.

What might be a few of your own physical restart rituals? These rituals don't have to be complicated or big. Think about the two taps on the heart that the Colorado State men's basketball team uses. What could you do to remind your mind and body to restart?

Your physical mistake rituals can be so subtle that people around you won't even know that you're performing them.

These reset rituals will help you mindfully start again quickly and get you back to doing what's truly important to you with compassion and kindness!

Living Your Way

People may tell you how to live your life—it's a given. Everyone has opinions about the best way to go about things, even other people's lives. But, you don't have to live your life according to other people's rules and ideas.

> You can live your way—that's the way that is in line with your valued path.

Sometimes, though, it's tricky and difficult to make important life choices and take action on them. Often we need a little helping hand and a reminder that we can do these hard things. At these times, we can learn to encourage ourselves and to tolerate the distress that shows up when we confront difficulties on our chosen life path.

PRACTICE #30:

See Your Future Self

To begin, let's make sure we are actually here and fully present. Start by slowing down your breathing. Breathing in through your nose to a count of five and out to a count of five. Do this for a minute or two and hear in your mind: slowing down, slowing down, slowing down. Often, we live in a virtual reality of our thoughts. Bringing our attention back to our breath helps us come back to what is actually happening here in the present.

Now that we have grounded ourselves in the present moment, imagine in the movie of your mind that you are walking down a hallway in your home. Suddenly, a door that has never been there before appears in front of you.

Curious, you open the door. As you walk into the room you find yourself surrounded by all the people and pets that have ever loved you. You may also see people in this room whom you have never met, but they are here because they have inspired you in some way. They are now here to support you just as your loved ones are here to support you.

As you enter the room, all of these people are lined up welcoming you and guiding you to another door farther into the room. Imagine their kind faces, the supportive tones of their voices, and the hugs and pats on the back they would give you as you walk through the room.

As you approach the next door you see light shining from it. As you open it you feel a welcoming warmth as you step in. Looking around you see you have stepped into your desired future life. You are invisible and you are watching your future self.

Watch closely to see what this future self does on a daily basis. What do you say or choose not to say? Watch how you walk, what you wear, the life and vitality in your skin and eyes. Notice where you live, who you are spending time with, what you do day to day, whether or not you have pets, how you travel from place to place. (Do you drive, walk, ride a bike, or take a bus or train?)

Soak in all the details of this future self.

What loving and supportive others were there for you when you walked through the mysterious door?

Now, imagine that this future self could come back to you in this present moment. Imagine what they would say to you to encourage you and comfort you. What gentle reminders would they have for you?

What internal barriers (tough thoughts and emotions) and external barriers (outside world stuff that's not in your head) would your future self help you deal with?

What advice would your future self give you for handling these challenges?

PRACTICE #31:

Stepping into Your Desired Future

Most of the practices we describe and talk about in this book can be done anywhere without anyone knowing what you are doing. This particular practice is a little different and really is best done where you can have some privacy and some space for walking around. You can even do this practice outside—perhaps in a yard or a park.

First, settle in on your desired space, then begin grounding yourself with our soothing rhythm breathing. Breathing in through the nose for five seconds and then breathing out for five seconds. Breathe this way until you feel a sense of calmness. Hear in your mind: slowing down, slowing down, slowing down; mind slowing down, body slowing down.

Once you have settled on your private space, look around you. As you look around imagine that your desired future is somewhere in front of you—where would it be? What part of the room or area (if you are outside) seems like the direction of your desired future? This may seem weird, but if you're willing to experiment, place your hand over your heart and walk to this place that feels most like your desired future life. (We place a hand or fist over our heart to remind us that we are following our heart and that our Compassionate Self is supporting us on this journey.)

> *Once you are at this desired future spot in the room or open space look around and notice how things look different from this perspective.*

Now walk slowly back to where you started as if you are your future self. Stand in front of where you originally started this practice. Close your eyes and imagine you could look into the eyes of your present self right now. As your future self, express your support, care, and wisdom. You may even want to reach out or give yourself a gentle hug to physically show your support rather than just your words.

Now open your eyes and sit down slowly in the place where you started. Let this experience soak into every cell of your body as if it could be recorded in your DNA.

Imagine that this experience has created an umbilical cord connection between this present moment and your desired future. Please remind yourself that with this exercise you are already heading in the right direction. Now you will be better equipped to recognize your path when you come across it in the future. You have been there before in your mind.

Courage

Taking steps toward your values takes courage!

Let's define courage first. When we talk about courage we are not talking about the kind of courage we see in movies, where it looks like the main characters never have fear. That's not really courage. The kind of courage we're talking about is the kind in which fear is acknowledged and embraced and then bold action is taken with fear going along for the ride!

So how do we take fear and its buddy the inner critic along for the ride?

The first step is to notice when fear is showing up. It can be tricky because both fear and the inner critic can sneak up on you through the backdoor or window of your life. When this happens, you can say, "Hello fear. I see you again (name it)."

Next you can chill fear out by slowing down your breathing. When you do this, fear may say

> "Don't do that! We might be in danger my friend!" Then take a pause and ask yourself, "Is what I am attempting to do truly important to me?"

If the answer is yes you then can imagine you are becoming your Compassionate Self. You adopt the physical posture of the Compassionate Self and then take just one positive action step. After you have completed that one small step, you take another small step, and another.

PRACTICE #32:

Leaning into Fear with and without Support

Stand with your feet together and imagine that ten feet in front of you is everyone and everything in the world that is truly important to you. Take a moment to really imagine all of these people, pets, and the things and places that are important to you. See their faces, their eyes, and hear the sound of their voices. Allow yourself to absorb their loving kindness (whether a person or an animal). See this scene in vivid detail in your mind.

Now physically lean your body slowly forward while keeping your feet cemented to the floor. If you feel comfortable, you can have a friend pretend to be your inner critic saying to you that you won't be able to lean like this and you should just stand still. Lean towards what is important to you until you fall forward.

Notice what happened. Did your foot step forward to save you before you fell on your face? Notice how this happened spontaneously as you continued to lean into your fear and towards what's important to you. Notice that there was a point at which—even with fearful thoughts— the momentum as you leaned forward carried you toward your values regardless of what fear had to say.

You can try this again but with your inner compassion coach whispering to you in your mind,

"It's ok fear. I'm leaning forward because what I see in front of me is important."

Notice the difference this time as compared to when you were just leaning forward as fear (or your inner critic) told you to stay still.

What did you notice? Was it easier for you the first time or the second time. What did fear do the first time as compared to the second time?

What might be one very small thing you can lean into today like this?

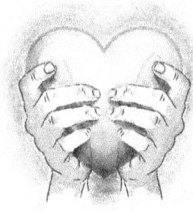

PRACTICE #33:

Creating Slowing-Down Rituals

As we have explored a little already,

sometimes you need to slow down in order to speed up.

You can't get ahead in life by only pushing and standing on your tiptoes all day long! Yes, there is a time for a little push and a time to stand on our tiptoes, but it isn't the most optimal mode for living our life on a daily basis.

Unfortunately, we often live under the assumption that we must push and strain 100% of the time to make any difference, to get ahead, and to reach our goals and dreams. Even if you have chilled-out parents who don't push, you're still swimming in a culture that sends this message all day long, every day.

There is a cultural vibe that if we are not in constant movement then we are doing something wrong. The art of slowing down to move ahead is not instinctive, but we can learn how to do it. When we push ourselves too hard all of the time, our Threat System can get overly activated and make it more difficult for us to take steps towards our values.

Starting to slow down can look different in different situations, but there are a few ways that we can easily tap into the slowing down mentality. These rituals work every time to help us slow down to speed up and activate our Drive System in a healthy way.

Breathing

As we have talked about throughout this book, mindful breathing is the foundation for everything. Slowing down is no different. It helps to ground us in the present moment, to bring mindful awareness, and gives us time to consider our next steps. For this reason, breathing is a great ritual to use before you are communicating with someone—especially over text. The next time you receive a text—especially one that might cause you to become worked up a bit over something—try this ritual:

⟡ When you hear the notification for your text, take one full deep breath before you look at the text.

⟡ Then, after you read the text, take a few slow deep breaths before responding to make sure you are really communicating clearly. This not only allows you to create a message that says what you want it to say, but also allows you to stay in alignment with your values.

Pausing and Purposely Taking More Time

This is a good ritual to use when you are trying to stay focused on a task at hand, like an assignment at school or for homework. Or even for an everyday activity that you would like to enjoy more. Sometimes when we speed through things we miss them completely and don't enjoy them as much.

Eating is a good example of an everyday activity where you could try this. Often we eat while we are on the move or while we are doing something else, such as watching TV, texting, etc. At your next meal, purposely choose to slow down by putting your electronics in another room.

As you begin your meal, give yourself the gift of slowing down by taking the first few bites while concentrating on the food in your mouth. What tastes are you experiencing: sweet, sour, salty? Is the food hot or cold? How do you feel as you are eating? This can just be a few moments—30 to 60 seconds—and it will make a difference.

Mindfully slowing down when you are eating allows you to savor (taste and enjoy) your food fully for a moment and it also allows you be aware of how much you're eating. Taking time to eat this way will help you to be able to listen to your body better, enjoy your food more, and in turn will help you know when you've had enough.

What does slowing down look like for you? Brainstorm some of your own slow-down rituals.

Your Personal Legend: Continue into the Future

By following the compass of your values, you are creating your personal legend. We usually think of legends as being people who do superhuman incredible things, and our thoughts may tell us that we are far from legendary. However, by following our values and by utilizing our strengths we are in fact creating our own personal legend!

When we are living out our personal legend, it inspires us and it also inspires the people around us. It's like an invisible ripple effect out into the world. You are both the hero and author of your own personal legend.

The journey begins this very moment, and if we stumble off the path of our personal legend we can always begin again with the compassionate mind skills we have developed.

Your contributions to the larger world are way more than you think and way more than you may ever know. The world needs you and your strengths. It needs all of you. Even those parts of you that appear to get in the way of your personal legend. This is the adventure of a lifetime and your personal legend will carry forward into the future to inspire others on their legendary path!

The Important Stuff

✧ Focus on your strengths. To identify some of your strengths, think about when you feel a sense of joy, accomplishment or pride. These things may even be challenging for you, but even in the challenge you are having fun or enjoying the process. In fact, an element of challenge that feels good is a sure sign that you are on the right path.

✧ Our gifts and our strengths are like a spark that can fire up our inspiration! This spark can give us the courage to go for what is really important to us and help us tolerate the discomfort that we will inevitably encounter on this path. Research has shown that people who identify their strengths and utilize them frequently in their lives experience greater well-being and happiness.

✧ With our Compassionate Self and Compassionate Other at our side, we can allow ourselves to explore. This may mean that we have success, but also that we allow ourselves to falter and then begin again and again in our pursuit of valued life direction, dreams, and goals. We can let go of unworkable thoughts and soothe difficult emotions as we pursue our life's greatest work.

✧ We can't be productive 100% of the time 24/7. The more we wear ourselves down by trying to be always productive, the more our minds become taken over by the Threat System. We will make more mistakes, get into more conflicts with others, and in general we will struggle more with the threat emotions of fear, anger, and sadness. An alternative is that we can learn to pursue our dream or our spark through soothing ourselves and then taking gradual purposeful steps. This type of committed action allows our minds and our bodies to respond with a sense of ease.

✧ When we learn to slow down we become more compassionate, creative, curious, and calm.

✧ By following the compass of your values you are creating your personal legend. When we are living out our personal legend, it inspires us and it also inspires the people around us. It's like an invisible ripple effect out into the world. The world needs you and your strengths. It needs all of you.

For more resources, guided practices, and meditations, please visit our website:
www.MindfulCompassionForTeens.com.

"As you get up in the morning, as you make decisions, as you spend money, make friends, make commitments, you are creating a piece of art called your life."

Mary Catherine Bateson

References & Resources
(Just so you know we didn't make all of this stuff up.)

The Compassionate Mind Foundation
https://compassionatemind.co.uk/about-us

The Center for Compassion Focused Therapy
http://www.mindfulcompassion.com/

Campbell, J. (1991). *The Power of Myth*. New York: Anchor, an imprint of Knopf Doubleday Publishing.

Edlund, M. (2011). *The Power of Rest: Why Sleep Alone Is Not Enough*. California: HarperOne.

Hanh, T. N. (2017). *The Art of Living: Peace and Freedom in the Here and Now*. California: HarperOne.

Hanh, T. N. (1992). *Peace is Every Step: The Path of Mindfulness in Everyday Life*. New York: Bantam Books.

Gilbert, P. (2009). *The Compassionate Mind*. London, United Kingdom: Constable & Robinson; Oakland, California: New Harbinger.

Gilbert, P. (2010). *Compassion Focused Therapy: The CBT Distinctive Features Series*. London: Routledge.

Hunter, M. R., Gillespie, B. W., & Chen, S. Y. Frontiers in Psychology (April 4, 2019). "Urban Nature Experiences Reduce Stress in the Context of Daily Life Based on Salivary Biomarkers"
https://doi.org/10.3389/fpsyg.2019.00722

Gilbert, P.; Choden. (2014). *Mindful Compassion: How the Science of Compassion Can Help You Understand Your Emotions, Live in the Present, and Connect Deeply with Others*. California: New Harbinger Publications, Inc.

Irons, C. (2018). *The Compassionate Mind Workbook: A Step-by-step Guide to Developing Your Compassionate Self*. London, United Kingdom: Constable & Robinson.

Kabat-Zinn, J. (1994). *Wherever You Go, There You Are: Mindfulness Meditation in Everyday Life*. New York: Hyperion.

Kolts, R. (2016). *CFT Made Simple: A Clinician's Guide to Practicing Compassion Focused Therapy*. California: New Harbinger Publications, Inc.

Marsh, I.C., Chan, S.W.Y. & MacBeth, A. Mindfulness (2018) 9: 1011. "Self-Compassion and Psychological Distress in Adolescents— a Meta-Analysis" https://link.springer.com/article/10.1007%2Fs12671-017-0850-7

Neff, K. (2011). *Self-Compassion: The Proven Power of Being Kind to Yourself*. William Morrow Paperbacks.

Seligman, M. E. P. (2012). *Flourish: A Visionary New Understanding of Happiness and Well-being*. New York: Atria Books.

Silberstein-Tirch, L. (2019). *How to Be Nice to Yourself: The Everyday Guide to Self-Compassion: Effective Strategies to Increase Self-Love and Acceptance*. California: Althea Press.

Tirch, D. D. (2012). *The Compassionate-Mind Guide to Overcoming Anxiety: Using Compassion-focused Therapy to Calm Worry, Panic, and Fear*. California: New Harbinger Publications, Inc.

Tirch, D.; Schoendorff, B.; Silberstein, L. (2014). *The ACT Practitioner's Guide to the Science of Compassion: Tools for Fostering Psychological Flexibility*. California: New Harbinger Publications, Inc.

Acknowledgements

First, we would like to thank all of the adolescents and teens who have had a hand in shaping this book. Each of you knows who you are and the special contributions you have made. Chris has worked with so many adolescents and teens over the course of the last 20 years and this book would have not been possible without all that we have learned from you! You have been the inspiration for this book and we are forever grateful to you for your courage, insights, dreams, vulnerability, tears, joy, music, laughter, curiosity, energy, perspective, and most of all your willingness to compassionately stretch beyond what you initially thought was possible for yourselves.

We would like to sincerely thank the reviewers and advanced readers of the book. Your feedback and encouragement was extremely helpful. Your insights really allowed us to hone our message for our readers in a way that wouldn't have been possible without you. Thank you Russell Kolts, Laura Silberstein-Tirch, Dennis Tirch, Sarah Cassidy, Tim Gordon, Katie Campbell, and Liz Brinkman.

We also want to acknowledge all the wonderful support, inspiration, and love we have received from Chris's CFT online supervision, and personal practice group facilitated by Dennis Tirch. Thank you Nancy Ring, Beth Fier, Greg Samuelson, Chia-Ying Chou, Carrie Diamond, Barry Sanders, Dave Rich, Linda Hamilton, Racheli Miller, Tina Siragusa, and Dennis Tirch. This book is imbued with your influence.

The art in this book is so very special, and we feel that the compassionate message we are sharing is stronger because of it. As we were thinking about the illustrations for this book at the beginning of the writing process we wanted to make sure that the art in the book would convey the compassion we feel in our hearts. Fortunately, we are blessed to be surrounded by so many talented people and we didn't have to look far to find the right artists for our message.

Thank you to Heather's high school friend Stephen Swartz, for stretching outside of your comfort zone to give us the most lovely series of compassionate hand illustrations. We hope that these illustrations will serve as a touchpoint and reminder for our readers that they are not alone as they move through the practices in the book and reflect on the content.

To Chris's amazing aunt, Heather Preston, you have given us the most beautiful gift with your art. We have dreamed of writing a book with your illustrations alongside our content and we are forever grateful to you for helping us make this dream come true in every way. Chris has been nurtured and comforted by your art his entire life and he is so pleased that we are now able to share it with adolescents. Your nature illustrations speak to us on such a deep level and we know that they will speak to our readers as well. Your life long mindfulness practice shines out through each illustration! Our gratitude is boundless.

To our interior and cover designers, Diane Six and Diane Lorenzo: thank you for sticking with us through this process and for bringing our vision to life. You really understood not only our message but also our readers as well.

To our copyeditor, Bridie O'Shaughnessy: we are so grateful for your attention to detail and your comments and feedback throughout the process. With you working on our book we could feel confident that no details would be lost. We truly appreciate your expertise and your steadfast friendship and belief in our compassionate message for teens.

Last but certainly not least, we would like to thank our families who have encouraged and supported us our entire lives. To our parents, Beth and Scott Fraser and Hilda and Francis Doyle. You have always been a shining example of what loving parents and marriage partners can be. Your steadfast love and care has made all the difference in our lives. Words are not enough to express our love and gratitude to you.

About the Authors

Photo Credit: Catherine Murray

Chris Fraser, MSW

Chris is the owner of Positive Path Counseling in Dublin, Ohio. Since 1996, he has served a variety of individual clients, couples, and families in both public and private settings. Chris has a passion for and an expertise in helping children, teens, and adults develop compassionate mind skills and how to use these skills to be the best versions of themselves.

Chris has over 20 years of experience and training in family therapy, acceptance and commitment therapy and compassion focused therapy. He works primarily from an authentic pairing of CFT (compassion focused therapy) and ACT (acceptance commitment therapy). Chris has been very fortunate to have trained with the creators of these therapeutic approaches and speaks on these topics locally, nationally, and internationally.

Chris loves the outdoors. He feels most at home running on wooded nature trails, swimming, downhill skiing, listening to music, dancing around the house with Heather, reading, traveling, and meeting amazing new people.

Heather Doyle Fraser

Heather is a coach, consultant, and author of multiple books including *40 Weeks: A Daily Journey of Inspiration and Abundance.* Heather is the owner of Beyond Change Coaching and Consulting in Dublin, Ohio. She utilizes compassionate mind training to help her coaching clients share their message and their voice whether they are in the board room, navigating a career change, or developing a book or other writing project. As an international coach, Heather is fortunate to work with individuals, small groups, and small businesses and also facilitates workshops and retreats. Heather holds space for her clients as they navigate change, achieve their goals, and create the success they envision for themselves.

In addition to coaching and writing, one of Heather's greatest joys in life is being able to sing and perform locally and nationally in the Ladies of Longford, a high-energy, all women contemporary Celtic band. This band has been performing since 2001 and is made up of her mother Hilda, her sister Stephanie, and dear friend Elizabeth.

Although this is their first book together, Heather and Chris enjoy working with each other on professional projects and are in the process of developing a compassionate mind wellness center in the midwest. They share an avid love of books, music, nature, good food, conversation, and of course their daughter. They enjoy spending time with their families whenever possible and reside in Dublin, Ohio.

About the Artists

Stephen Swartz

Stephen Swartz was born in Columbus, Ohio in 1973. He attended the Columbus College of Art and Design from 1991—1997 and graduated with a B.F.A. in Media Studies. A photographic artist, illustrator, and designer, Swartz is primarily known for his abstract analog photography. Influenced by his love of architecture, he juxtaposes the softness of the human form with the hard shapes and geometric structures of buildings and small rigid spaces. Thus, he has been afforded the opportunity to participate in several Urban Art experiences. In 2005, Swartz left Columbus and moved to Europe in order to broaden his creative horizons within the context of the 'Old World'. He currently lives in Germany with his wife and two children.

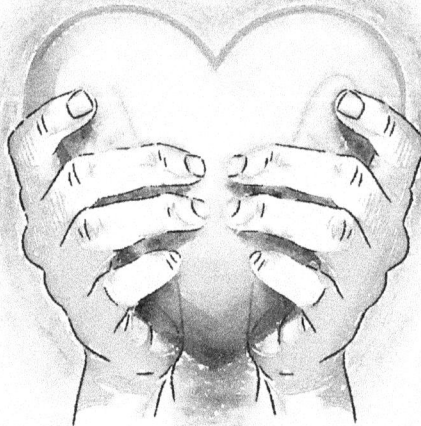

Heather Preston

Heather Preston was born and educated in Chicago, Illinois. She graduated with honors and distinction from The Art Institute of Chicago and was named one of Chicago's outstanding artists. She has exhibited in art galleries across the United States, taught fine art classes, has won many awards for her work in general and also as a book illustrator and commercial art illustrator. Preston has studied throughout Europe and the world. She moved to San Francisco in 1970 and still resides in this area. Recently, she won a silver literary medal for her book *Tree Spirits: Tales and Encounters* published in 2009. Preston is a lifelong learner of culture and society whose interests include meditation and world peace.